ARCHITECTS' DREAM HOUSES

JEAN-CLAUDE DELORME

PHOTOGRAPHY BY THIBAUT CUISSET

ABBEVILLE PRESS PUBLISHERS   NEW YORK   LONDON   PARIS

To Jacques Dubois

Front cover: South elevation of the Hill House, Glasgow,
designed by Charles Rennie Mackintosh (see also page 26).
Back cover: A picture window in Villa Malaparte, Capri,
designed by Emmanuel Pontremoli (see also page 111).

Translated from the French by Willard Wood

English-language edition
Editor: Jacqueline Decter
Text and jacket Designer: Molly Shields
Production Editor: Owen Dugan
Production Assistant: Becky Boutch

First edition
10 9 8 7 6 5 4 3 2 1

Library of Congress Cataloging-in-Publication Data
Delorme, Jean-Claude.
    [Maisons d'exception. English]
    Architects' dream houses / Jean-Claude Delorme ; photography by
Thibaut Cuisset ; translated from the French by Willard Wood.
        p.   cm.
        ISBN 0-7892-0127-5 (hc.) — ISBN 0-7892-0126-7 (pbk.)
        1. Architects—Homes and haunts. 2. Architect-designed houses.
I. Title.
NA7195.A7D4513   1996
728′.092′24—dc20   95-50841

CONTENTS

PREFACE

It would be impossible, in telling the story of a few exceptional houses, to give an idea of architecture as a whole during the closing years of the nineteenth century. It was an ambiguous era, one in which new values were being sought and many styles flourished side by side before the great cataclysm of 1914 and the radical revolutions in aesthetics that followed.

The richness of these houses, their preciosity of style, and their exuberance of form are the product of an intellectual moment somewhere between the dominant historicism of the nineteenth century and the rationalism then coming into being with the widespread creation of industrial spaces.

These fin de siècle houses are neither caricatures of a classical style nor manifestos embodying a new ordering of space; they are first and foremost the expression of strong individualities in search of a harmonious world. They represent the final form of a story, or of stories, in which the unconscious and the conscious have embarked on a complex and sometimes contradictory undertaking.

Before modernism's inexorable wave swept over the world, before white walls and a lack of ornament came to express a new era, these exceptional houses bespoke an authentic intellectual adventure. And before one-dimensional men were programmed from birth in architecture that was a virtual "machine for living," there were the architectural productions of artists at the end of the nineteenth century, which seem to me to open roads to freedom that have as yet not been explored. These homes collectively belong to no dominant style, no cultural hegemony, and no official movement; each brings attention to its own differences, and each is a unique gesture, an exceptional gesture. In their own way, they are all rejections of the houses of the time; they represent the search for a new truth, but none naively proclaims its style or its values as supreme.

Ornament, at times overabundant, is the telltale sign of fin de siècle architecture. The frenzied effort to qualify every surface, and to inscribe every space, would lead Adolf Loos to declare that "ornament is a crime."

Once the message was adopted by the Bauhaus of Walter Gropius and amplified in the abundant writings of Le Corbusier, the impulse to be modern became a frantic necessity—and the modern aesthetic made the eradication of any personal expression an absolute imperative. The time for dreams was over, the fictions of history were abolished, and with only pure volumes in broad daylight remaining, the intensive production of new and modern spaces could begin.

The Villa Kerylos, Sir John Soane's house, Sir Edwin Lutyens's Mallet House, the Güell Palace, and the Hill House—each in its own way raises the question of ornament.

When the architect Emmanuel Pontremoli received the commission for the Villa Kerylos from Theodore Reinach in 1902, his task was to build a Greek villa. In 1904, when Adolf Loos designed a villa in Montreux for Dr. Beer, he deliberately kept it extremely naked. Then how could it be that the two houses show disturbing analogies? How could it be that Pontremoli and Loos, despite their totally different historical references, possessed and implemented highly comparable concepts of design? They both resort to symmetry, to an interior court, to the notion of order, to a ground floor, main body, and attic, and to punctuating the corners with a square or round tower—all correspondences that are deeply troubling. There are equally surprising analogies between Le Corbusier's Villa Savoye (1929) and Andrea Palladio's Villa Rotonda (1569): why do both villas have such similar façades, open on all four sides around a central plan?

It is odd that the quintessential Le Corbusier villa should hark back to Palladio, when the modern master was so adamant in refusing to use the styles of the past, remarking that "a style is like the plume on a lady's hat." And why should Adolf Loos, entering a design in the Chicago Tribune Tower competition, propose a monumental Doric column on a heavy plinth?

How could it be that one of the greatest architects of the twentieth century, Louis Kahn, based all his work on a return to architectural archetypes? The National Assembly complex at Dacca, the capital of Bangladesh, which he designed in 1962, uses only pure forms: the cube, the circle, and the pyramid. Kahn's work expresses the recent profound change in architectural culture: all styles, even that of the rationalist movement, have been replaced by a new formalism.

Kahn's projects are based on a philosophy of architecture shot through with religion and metaphysics. They are acts of the spirit, in which form is no longer fitted exclusively to function but expresses philosophical values.

When Curzio Malaparte built his house on a rocky spit facing the Mediterranean, his choice of architect was Adalberto Libera, a man who defended modernism and rationality from his base in Rome. Malaparte chose the pure form of a rectangular parallelepiped. The straight lines and plane surfaces of the cubist box he daringly set down on rock are in stark contrast to the luxuriant vegetation, the rocks, and the horizon. Yet the writer was not satisfied with his cube; he built onto it a staircase that widens as it rises, looking startlingly like a Greek theater, and reaches a crescendo at the level of the roof terrace, where the awestruck spectator discovers the grand spectacle of the sea. For the walls, Malaparte rejected the dazzling white urged by the modernist Libera and chose a Pompeian red, a red that reminds one of the surfaces of Rome and of those ruined towns under the ashes. Malaparte, a contemporary novelist who saw himself as the bard of a triumphant modernism, built a house for himself that is anciently modern, mixing two styles, two epochs, and two emotions—those of the past and those of the present.

This house is in some sense a concrete metaphor for our era, which to advance has an ineluctable need of the past. Our most original awareness of modernity, felt as the need to go toward the new and the unknown, unconsciously feeds, whatever may have been said or written about it, on the past. This past is our culture; these houses tell us stories and in their own way express the contradiction every creator faces.

The sculptor Phidias, the painter Giotto, Michelangelo, and the architects Soane, Pontremoli, Loos, Le Corbusier, and Kahn—each in turn raises the same question of his relation to history. Each defines his position in his own way, and the artist who claims to have no debt to history simply reveals his rash megalomania. There is no escaping history, and all who express their freedom by a violent break with tradition unconsciously base their work on what has come down to us from classical antiquity and use its graphic forms. For a creative artist, the dilemma is that others before have lived out the same adventure: that of breaking free of the past.

THE HOUSE OF SIR JOHN SOANE

LONDON

Soane's work belongs in a transitional moment after the neoclassical period of the eighteenth century and before the eclecticism of the nineteenth. Although he remained attached to the rules and conventions of neoclassical architecture, Soane borrowed freely from the architecture of Greece, Rome, the Middle Ages, and the Baroque period. His ties to classical antiquity and his manner of copying the ancients led him to explore all the facets of what proved a uniquely personal style. A particular influence on Soane was Giovanni Battista Piranesi (1720–1778), whose vision of Rome would influence the classical revival movement throughout Europe. Another strong influence was the abbé Marc-Antoine Laugier (1713–1769), a great theorist of eighteenth-century architecture whose writings urged the use of simple geometrical forms.

Architect
JOHN SOANE

THE FORMATIVE YEARS

Soane was born in Goring, a small village on the Thames, in 1753. His father was a bricklayer, and John was the youngest of seven children. At the age of fifteen, after completing secondary school, he met an assistant to the architect George Dance and was accepted into his London office as a junior assistant.

In 1776, when Soane was twenty-three, he received a gold medal from the Royal Academy of Arts for his design for a triumphal bridge. He was then presented to the king by the neoclassical architect Sir William Chambers (1723–1796), a tutor to the Prince of Wales on architectural subjects and the dowager princess's personal architect. This led to Soane's receiving a royal fellowship for two years of study in Italy. From 1778 to 1780 he toured Italy and Sicily, where he met the engraver Piranesi, who was to have such an influence on his future work.

In 1781 Soane began his professional career. He opened an office in London and designed his first houses in the east of England. All of Soane's houses were built with great attention to detail, and the remarkable state of preservation of Shotesham Park gives evidence of the quality of his work and the rigor of its ornamentation. The plans for the many buildings he designed and restored are collected in two books, *Plans, Elevations and Sections of Buildings Erected in the Counties of Norfolk, Suffolk, . . .* (1788) and *Sketches in Architecture* (1793). The influence of the French school is very marked, as is his early interest in the lighting effects produced by glass domes and cupolas.

But it was his appointment in 1788 as architect to the Bank of England, a position he would hold until 1833, that was the true point of departure for his creative work. He began in 1790 by remodel-

ing the bank's interior, immediately showing his innovativeness by abandoning the current heavy, classical manner and replacing it with his own inimitable, extremely graphic style. An enormous glass cupola resting on caryatids and on four vaults with pendentive arches provides lighting from above, an effect reinforced by the high, windowless walls. This is the start of Soane's exploration of light. In this vast complex, which he would rework over the next forty-five years, he would have ample opportunity to explore a multitude of spatial combinations.

SOANE'S HOUSE

In 1784 Soane married Eliza Smith. The marriage was a happy one, and produced two sons. When Eliza's uncle left them his fortune in 1790, the couple's financial security was assured, and in 1792 the architect, then thirty-nine years old, was able to start building the house at 12 Lincoln's Inn Fields that would hold both the family quarters and his professional offices. In 1808 he bought the adjoining lot at no. 13, where he installed his library and dining room. The extension also included the Dome Room and two new floors on which he would establish his architectural office. The third phase of construction occurred in 1812, when Soane built the triple loggia, which he called the veranda, on the front façade in Portland stone. The fourth and last phase began in 1824 when Soane, then seventy-one years old, bought and tore down the building at no. 14 and completely restructured the backs of lots 12 and 13 to house his museum, consisting of the new picture room and the Monk's Parlour. From the time the first lot was purchased in 1792 until the completion of the museum in 1825, more than thirty years had elapsed.

The architect's goal, which he achieved perfectly, was to build over time a coherent whole where he could display his many collections, and to leave his own house, a virtual manifesto of the art of living, as his final architectural message.

THE FRONT FAÇADE

Characteristic of Soane's domestic architecture is its discretion—there is no attempt made for the house to stand out at all costs from its neighbors. The principles evident in the front elevation of Soane's house are those he had used previously in the façade of Pitzhanger Manor. A central stone element is framed by two lateral wings made of brick, and a succession of diminishing volumes accentuates the effect of height. Soane appreciated the result of offsetting an ornamental stone structure against a background of brickwork. The three-bay central loggia consists of an entry floor, a main level with three arched

Opposite: The façade of
13 Lincoln's Inn Fields, London.

windows, and two upper stories that are recessed from the main level. The house follows the rule of the English court in being built back from the street to provide illumination for the service areas located in the cellar.

THE LIBRARY AND DINING ROOM

One enters through a narrow entrance hall, its walls painted in an imitation of porphyry. From there one proceeds immediately to the dining room, an enormous rectangular area lit by daylight filtering in through the library. It is the largest space in the house, divided into two parts by a curious hanging triple arch in the Gothic style. In English houses, the "modern" practice was to use the library as a living room. This ceremonial room, known as the "great parlor," was designed to be distinct and set off on its own. The new conception, implemented by Soane, was to open the library onto the dining room so that the warmth of the wainscoting and the books would be communicated to the room where one ate.

Natural light also enters the house by reflection off the many mirrors, which both raise the level of light in the rooms and increase their apparent size. When the tax on windows was lowered in 1815, it became possible to increase the size of windows and rely more on daylight; at the same time, the use of metal in construction allowed the gradual replacement of thick wooden windows by thinner openings. Houses were undergoing a revolutionary transformation at the beginning of the nineteenth century, and the evidence is manifest in Soane's house.

THE CORRIDOR

Before entering the picture room, one proceeds along a narrow corridor lit from above by a glass skylight. Originally the glass was tinted yellow, as can be seen in the views of the house painted by Soane's faithful collaborators, Charles J. Richardson and George Bailey. This collection of 125 watercolors enables us to know and study the house as it appeared on its completion in 1830. The walls of the corridor are hung with plaster casts of funerary urns, friezes, cornices, and an array of decorative elements indispensable to an eighteenth-century architect. Most of the objects on display today have been there since they were originally hung.

THE DRAWING OFFICE

Two skylights provide vertical illumination for this small room, furnished with a number of drafting tables, which was established for Soane's draftsmen in 1821 and rebuilt in 1824. On the walls are classical motifs, which served as models. The drawers are full of architectural drawings intended for the edification of young apprentices, among them a superb *View of the Bank of England* by Joseph Michael Gandy (1771–1843), one of Soane's principal collaborators.

Six draftsmen worked in this room. They arrived at 9:00 A.M. and entered their work in registers belonging to the studio. These registers are still preserved in the museum, along with more than eight thousand drawings and sketches: every step of each project has been kept, along with the models that were made for it. It was the first time that such complete documentation of an eighteenth-century architectural practice was assembled.

THE PICTURE ROOM

This is the most exceptional space, with its large pivoting panels on which the collection of Piranesi's works is displayed. Soane met Piranesi in 1778, the year of the great architect's death, and received four drawings from him that formed the start of a collection Soane would complete in the course of his travels. There are also Romantic paintings by Joseph Mallord William Turner and William Hogarth, a beautiful study for the ceiling of Hampton Court Palace by Sir John Thornhill dating from 1715, and a watercolor of Soane's country house, Pitzhanger Manor, painted by J. M. Gandy. The visit ends with the moving panels being opened to display the entirety of their wonders to the public eye. As if by magic, the last panels open onto emptiness, and daylight floods the space.

THE BREAKFAST ROOM

On the subject of the breakfast room, Sir John Soane wrote, "The views from this room into the Monument Court and the Museum, the mirrors in the ceiling, and the looking glasses, combined with the variety of outline and general arrangement and the design and decoration of this limited space, present a succession of those fanciful effects which constitute the poetry of architecture." This square room is topped by a shallow dome resting on four pendentives inset with mirrors. Soane finds a congruence here with the Baroque architecture of Bavaria and the art of Johann Balthasar Neumann or the Asam brothers, Cosimo Damian and Egid Quinn. He brings in natural light through the periphery of the vault and reduces the supports to a minimum to produce an effect of extreme lightness. Soane manages to avoid any impression of weight, achieving the airy grace of a magician. The numerous convex mirrors emphasize the feeling of immateriality, the breaking up of light and space. The breakfast room shows that it is possible to introduce light even into a small room at the heart of a vast dwelling with three windowless walls; in fact, light shines throughout the house.

Soane was among the first to establish a new relation to the classical tradition. None understood better than he Piranesi's message that light and dark might constitute a new material for an architecture of the emotions. Soane's architecture is not the simple assemblage of elements under light but the work of a magician. It provides a lesson for today's architects, who tend to reduce a house to a machine for living. As early as the eighteenth century, Soane had shown that a house can be a machine for dreaming.

The library and dining room.

A detail of the ceiling arch in the library.

*Opposite: A copy of the Apollo Belvedere
under the vertical lighting of the dome.*

*View from under the dome of
the breakfast room.*

The vertically lit drawing office.

Opposite: After the light, the obscurity of the crypt.

RED HOUSE

BEXLEYHEATH, KENT

Although Great Britain was the greatest industrial power in the nineteenth century, it was there that the Domestic Revival, or Arts and Crafts movement, arose. Industrialization transformed the appearance of both town and countryside, and writers, painters, and architects reacted strongly to what they considered the destruction of English culture.

The political stability of England under Queen Victoria, who reigned from 1837 to 1901, fostered the largest industrial revolution any country had experienced; the British, for all their attachment to tradition, saw their countryside thrown into turmoil and their towns slashed by roads and railway stations and invaded by enormous factories. In 1851 the first Great Exhibition was held in London to celebrate the triumphs of science, technology, and the arts throughout the industrial world.

JOHN RUSKIN (1819–1900)

John Ruskin, who led the charge against the idol of Progress, was born in 1819 and died insane in 1900, the same year as Friedrich Nietzsche. Like many other intellectuals, he took exception to the brutal changes England was undergoing, and it was he who spearheaded the reaction against Victorian style and its taste for excess. He believed that industrialization leads to a dehumanizing mechanical perfection, in contrast to the production of craftsmen, which might have imperfections but expresses the human soul and its sensibility. His theories were to influence an entire generation of writers, artists, and architects—among them William Morris, a socialist and the founder, moral conscience, and theoretician of the Arts and Crafts movement, whose aesthetic aimed at providing a clearheaded reaction to the nefarious consequences of unbridled industrialization.

WILLIAM MORRIS (1834–1896)

A typical British intellectual of the Victorian era, Morris was of middle-class origins. He attended Oxford in the 1850s, when Ruskin was having an enormous impact on artistic, spiritual, and political education. A socialist businessman, Morris was one of the first to create a bridge between the worlds of art and work. At Oxford, where he was to meet his lifelong friend Edward Burne-Jones, he read *The Stones of Venice* (1851–53), which Ruskin had just published and which included "The Nature of the Gothic." This work had a decisive influence on the fate of the two young men: Burne-Jones went on to become a painter; Morris, an architect. In 1857 the two were living together at 17 Red Lion Square; unable to find any furniture that was to his

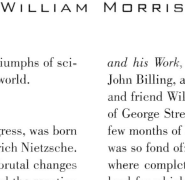

WILLIAM MORRIS

liking, Morris designed a few massive pieces, which he had built by a local carpenter and then decorated himself with paintings drawn from Chaucer and Dante. Thus was "savage" furniture born.

RED HOUSE (1859)

The architect of Red House was Philip Webb (1831–1915), who was born in the town of Oxford and whose entire childhood passed in the shadow of its handsome Gothic architecture. Architect and writer William Richard Lethaby quoted him as saying, "I had no other teacher in art than the impressive objects of the old buildings, the effect of which on my natural bent has never left me" (*Philip Webb and his Work*, 1935). From 1849 to 1852 Webb was apprenticed to John Billing, an architect in Reading. In 1856 he met his future client and friend William Morris while they were both working in the offices of George Street. He designed Red House at Bexleyheath in the first few months of 1859. It was one of those beautiful sites William Morris was so fond of: "The English countryside is the place above all others where complete harmony obtains between the works of men and the land for which they were destined. . . . Everything in it is measured, mixed and varied; one thing melts harmoniously into another. Small rivers, small plains. . . . Everything is polished, without ever being clumsy or superfluous. In fact, all is of the greatest seriousness and charged with meaning for any who take the trouble to seek for it. Neither a prison nor a palace, it is an honest dwelling" (conference on the minor arts, 1877).

In designing this house, Webb used a style that is bare of all ornament and makes no explicit reference to the Gothic Revival architecture sweeping London at the time, as the new Parliament buildings were undergoing reconstruction. The use of red brick rather than stone, the absence of projecting elements, and the avoidance of any symmetry or pronounced compositional axis all point to an explicit distancing from Victorian architecture. Webb drew his inspiration from Ruskin's ideal of a return to the primitive simplicity of rural construction. The pivot of his design is the corner tower, and the house's L-shaped plan is organized around it.

There is a trace of Gothic style in the roofs, which are steeply pitched and topped by a lantern, and in the ogives over the windows and loggia. For the roofing, Webb chose to use red slate, giving a monochromatic effect that emphasizes the building's massiveness. The red brick and slate reinforce the unity and strength of the composition. The size and proportions of the openings further emphasize the massiveness,

Opposite: The simplicity of the large gable wall of red brick and slate.

while their free placement follows the interior functions of the spaces. The fenestration is in fact highly varied: there are vertical sash windows, circular ones, others with ogival arches over them, and dormer windows in the roof.

Webb innovated by replacing the usual configuration of one room leading into another with a series of independent rooms set out along a long hallway. In this way he created an L-shaped plan that allowed him to design a small interior courtyard with a well in the center, a necessity as there were no water mains. This basic design would be used time and again in Arts and Crafts houses until the end of the nineteenth century. The main public spaces—the drawing room and dining room—face north, while the kitchen and bedrooms face west.

The interior decoration of the house is sober: wood, brick, the wallpapers of William Morris, paintings by Burne-Jones and Dante Gabriel Rossetti, and the massive furniture designed by Webb and Morris. The windows of the gallery are of stained glass, after designs by Morris and Webb, and bear the motto SI JE PUIS ("If I Can") against a background of floral motifs. The fireplace, designed by the architect, anticipates in its simplicity the designs of Lutyens. Instead of a massive lintel supported by straight, heavy legs there is a single handsome brick chimneypiece. The bricks are laid horizontally in the hearth and vertically in the design of the hood. A light frieze reminds us that art is eternal and life short. The fireplace is entirely functional, and is derived from no known style.

The great staircase, which occupies a square stair space, is made of oak. Above the stairwell, in the corner tower, is what Lawrence Weaver called "a tall pyramidal roof, left open on the inside and patterned in blue and green, a little Persian in feeling" (*Small Country Houses of Today*). Daylight enters through a small lantern in the center. Webb even designed the dishes and cutlery, as Morris could find nothing on the market that met his exacting standards. In the drawing room on the second floor is a large chest with doors decorated by Burne-Jones and a central panel painted with a *Dantis amor* by Rossetti. The raftered ceiling was to have had frescoes by Burne-Jones, but only three of the seven scenes from the romance of Sir Degrevaunt were completed—the three in which Morris and his wife are depicted as the medieval Sir Degrevaunt and his bride. A young architect named C. R. Ashbee was once invited to the Morris household and commented, "[William Morris] received us kindly and invited us all in to supper. Everything in the house is beautiful—such Rossettis, and such a harmony of color and tones! Miss Morris in a plain crimson velvet dress with red glass beads and a silver ornament, looked like an Italian chatelaine of the fifteenth century. Sitting at table one felt like one of the people in Millais's Pre-Raphaelite picture of Isabella. Everything harmonious . . ."

MORRIS'S FIRM IN 1861

Red House was truly a collective work, and its creation and construction were decisive experiences in William Morris's career, as he thereby became an interior designer and decorator. Leaving architectural design to Webb, Morris took up the design of furniture, wallpaper, fabrics, and table services in April 1861.

As Red House was being completed, the firm of Morris, Marshall, Faulkner and Co. was created to supply the public with new craftwork articles. It opened at 8 Red Lion Square and offered furniture, paintings, stained glass, embroidery, tableware, and sculptures. The items that would make it prosper, however, were the wallpapers and cotton fabrics printed with floral motifs. William Morris rejected any large-scale industrialization, and the cotton cloth continued to be hand printed from engraved wooden blocks. The company was also the first to forge links between the world of art and the world of business—in making these objects of domestic art, the artists and artisans who designed them became aware that a strong thread links art, aesthetics, and industrial production. There should not be an art for the elite on the one hand and manufactured articles of mediocre quality on the other; instead, the artist owes it to himself to apply aesthetic criteria to the greatest possible number of objects.

With the creation in 1884 of the Central School of Arts and Crafts, founded by William Richard Lethaby, a direct disciple of William Morris, and the London Exposition of 1888, where the Arts and Crafts Society displayed its works, Morris's innovative ideas began to spread throughout Europe.

The influence of the Arts and Crafts movement thus reached beyond the borders of Victorian England and was felt in Germany, Holland, France, the Scandinavian countries, and all the way to the United States. All of these countries were receptive to the idea of a return to simplicity in architecture and the decorative arts.

Robie House (1906), built in Chicago by Frank Lloyd Wright, was directly inspired by the Arts and Crafts movement. The dominant horizontality of its lines, its massive chimney and large roof structures, the use of brick, and the rejection of ornament and corbeled roofs all point to the influence of the British school on the American. John Ruskin's *Seven Lamps of Architecture* (1849) was one of the first books that Wright read, and Morris was one of the heroes of his youth. Frank Lloyd Wright would in fact deliver a lecture at Hull House called "The Art and Craft of the Machine."

Red House is clearly an emblematic work—the first strong and vigorous expression of the principles of the modern movement in architecture and the decorative arts. And in spite of the heaviness of its lines, it remains an honest and authentic expression of a new moral imperative. Red House, which refers back to the aesthetics of the Middle Ages and echoes the spirit of Eugène Emmanuel Viollet-le-Duc, represents a crucial stage in the development of a new aesthetic based on principles of austerity and simplicity. It is the work of craftsmen, but rises through the many ideals embodied in it to the level of an exceptional work of art.

Opposite: The front door is decorated with
geometrical motifs by William Morris.

The walls and ceiling of the stairwell are covered with wallpapers by the Morris firm.

Opposite: Romanesque and Gothic arches in the north wing.

*In the entryway is a chest of
Pre-Raphaelite inspiration,
painted by William Morris.*

The fireplace in the second-floor drawing room.

*Paintings by Edward Burne-Jones (right) and Dante Gabriel Rossetti (left)
hang in the second-floor drawing room.*

THE HILL HOUSE

GLASGOW

Architect

C. R. MACKINTOSH

Scottish architect Charles Rennie Mackintosh was born in Glasgow in 1868, the second in a family of eleven children. His career was relatively brief, as barely twenty years elapsed between his first projects in 1893 and the close of his professional activities in 1913. In that time he built two country houses, a church, a school, several tea rooms, and his masterpiece, the Glasgow School of Art.

Relatively little known in his own country during his lifetime, he owes his fame to German and Austrian architects, particularly the members of the Vienna Secession, who recognized him as the true precursor of the modern movement in Great Britain.

After the wave of the Arts and Crafts movement, which carried the resurgence of the English aesthetic from 1860 on, it was Mackintosh's Glasgow School of Art project that provided the reference point for a transition to the modern movement in Austria and Germany. Viennese masters such as Otto Wagner, Josef Hoffmann, and Adolf Loos would draw many references from the work of the great Scottish designer. Mackintosh was the first to break with Art Nouveau's curvilinearity, resolutely turning toward an elegant geometrical style in which ornament is secondary to the clear expression of spatial structure. It is astonishing to note how a body of work as local and as modest as Mackintosh's was able to exert the seductive influence that it did.

THE FORMATIVE YEARS

At sixteen Mackintosh joined the architectural offices of John Hutchison as an apprentice, taking evening courses at the Glasgow School of Art, an institution to which he retained ties for more than fifteen years. A refined designer and tireless worker, he was awarded many prizes for projects ranging in style from Gothic to Renaissance. In 1890 he received a fellowship to study in France and Italy; on his return in 1891, he held a conference on Scottish feudal architecture. At twenty-one he joined the firm of Honeyman and Keppie as a draftsman, meeting there his future brother-in-law, Herbert McNair. At art school, the two friends made the acquaintance of their wives-to-be, Margaret and Frances Macdonald, two sisters who worked in watercolors, embroidery, graphic design, and metal embossing.

Francis Newbery, president of the School of Art from 1885 on, was to radically transform what had been a technical design school for artisans, including ironworkers, cabinetmakers, and designers. Changing the content and intellectual level of the syllabus, he opened the school to the avant-garde movements of Europe and invited many of the prime instigators of the Vienna Secession.

Newbery encouraged his most brilliant students—Mackintosh, McNair, and the Macdonald sisters—to form a group and exhibit their first works, under the name of the Glasgow Four, at the Arts and Crafts Exhibition Society in London in 1896. They were warmly acclaimed as the "Spook School" by Gleeson White, editor of the famous review the *Studio,* which would become the magazine of reference for innovators in aesthetics. The magazine's first issue in 1893 featured three drawings by Aubrey Beardsley, who would illustrate Oscar Wilde's *Salomé,* published in 1894. Beardsley developed a stylized graphic manner inspired by Japanese art, whose nervous and supple line prefigured Art Nouveau. Pre-Raphaelite artists such as Edward Burne-Jones and Dante Gabriel Rossetti considerably influenced the Glasgow Four. Reacting against Victorian academicism and the ills of industrial society, the Pre-Raphaelite movement marked a return to natural forms and a reappreciation of the Middle Ages and the Italian primitives. The symbolism found in the watercolors of the Macdonald sisters and in the posters designed by Mackintosh and McNair confirm their strong inclination toward the esoteric and the use of forms that symbolized nature. In 1895 Francis Newbery proposed that the art school he was in the process of transforming be provided with a new building. An architectural contest was held, and eleven designs were submitted, with first place going to the firm of Honeyman and Keppie for the designs of its twenty-eight-year-old architect Charles Rennie Mackintosh.

FIRST WORKS

The first work for which Mackintosh was responsible within his architectural firm was the enlargement of the Glasgow Herald building, a six-story corner building in the center of Glasgow. Mackintosh would raise a great nine-story tower of medieval inspiration to articulate the two street-facing façades. In 1897 Mackintosh designed the Presbyterian Queen's Cross Church, which falls well within the Gothic Revival style in England. It included a massive, square corner tower, again articulating the two street façades; one enters the church through this combination bell tower and porch. The nave is covered by a vaulted ceiling set within a wooden frame; each of the side walls culminates in an upper gallery. It is a modest building, but the architect took great care in designing every aspect of the interior: the pulpit, wall paneling, upper gallery, altar, choir, and pews are all delicately designed and decorated with fine arabesques bearing regular striations and crowned with stylized roses.

In 1904–6 Mackintosh designed the very

Opposite: The large white gable wall and round tower of the south elevation.

handsome Scotland Street School. Situated on the left bank of the Clyde, in a working quarter on the outskirts of downtown Glasgow, it accommodated 1,250 students in twenty-one classrooms. The architect erected a red sandstone façade 164 feet (50 meters) long on Scotland Street, flanked by two cylindrical staircase towers hollowed out to their full height. Here also the reference to a medieval castle is explicit in the massive, vertical round towers, their turrets completely covered in small, square, leaded windowpanes.

THE GLASGOW SCHOOL OF ART

When the school received a gift of land on Sauchiehall Street from a philanthropist in 1895, Newbery announced the design competition. The first phase of building started in 1899 with the construction of the studios and the main entrance facing north on Sauchiehall Street. Ten years later the second phase was completed with the building of the library. Given the massive height of the west façade, accentuated by the steeply dropping street, this would be the project's most spectacular element. Pushing this façade's monumentality to the limit, the architect designed three narrow, twenty-five-foot-high windows to light the library from floor to ceiling. We are a long way here from Art Nouveau arabesques. Drawing on the massive, heavy Scottish castle, Mackintosh succeeded in creating a work that is emblematic of the modern movement.

Thus, in less than ten years, and working on the same project, the architect abandoned his light graphic style for what amounts to architectural dramaturgy. After designing several tea rooms, a church, and two country houses, Mackintosh culminated his architectural career with the building of the School of Art library. He and his wife sold their house in Glasgow in 1919, settling in Port-Vendres, France, in 1923, where the architect devoted himself to painting oils and watercolors. Mackintosh died of throat cancer in London in 1928.

THE HILL HOUSE (1902–4)

Charles Rennie Mackintosh would create two large country houses on hilltops: Windyhill (1890–1901) at Kilmacolm, Renfrewshire, and the Hill House (1902–4) at Helensburgh, Dunbartonshire. These two houses, very similar in design, were inspired by eighteenth-century Scottish architecture, as well as by the Arts and Crafts movement. According to Francis Newbery, Mackintosh's teacher at the Glasgow School of Art, the country houses of C. F. A. Voysey (1857–1941) were Mackintosh's main inspiration.

In Helensburgh, an elegant suburb twenty-five miles to the west of Glasgow, the industrialist Walter Blackie bought a spectacular piece of land on a hilltop overlooking the Firth of Clyde. The scion of a wealthy family of Glasgow publishers, Blackie wanted a seventeen-room country house where he might live with his four children and seven servants.

Faithful to the Arts and Crafts tradition, Mackintosh selected an L-shaped plan. All the reception areas were on the ground floor, whereas the more than seven bedrooms and the service areas were grouped on the floor above.

Though the exterior of the house might remind one of a Scottish manor house, Mackintosh has made the lines purer, his concessions to tradition being the large chimneys and round towers. Indoors, the spare lines and radically new vocabulary of this great designer of the late nineteenth century are plainly manifest. The Japanese influence is evident in the austerity of the dark woodwork and in the all-powerful geometry that orders, rules, and compartmentalizes the house. The carpets, windows, lamps, doors, and woodwork are all ornamented with squares—the veritable logo of the Mackintosh style.

After climbing the four steps of the large entry hall, the visitor emerges from the dark ambience initially greeting him to find himself between the white walls of the drawing room. This space, the single largest in the house, consists of a corner with a fireplace, a music alcove, and a banquette that runs the length of a large, south-facing horizontal window bay. There is also a hidden side door to the garden, just as in Lutyens's Varengeville house. The diaphanous daylight is filtered through superb white curtains designed by Margaret Macdonald and reflected in a fireplace faced with mosaic and inset with white and pink ellipses—a technique regularly used by the Arts and Crafts movement in place of wallpaper or a tapestry. In designing the office, Mackintosh lined the room with dark wooden bookcases, on the shelves of which the master of the house could display the entire output of his publishing house. The dining room is paneled in black wood, while a golden geometric lamp, inlaid with pink glass, hangs above the varnished table. In the great round tower is a majestic staircase, its two flights separated by a thin openwork wood partition and culminating in a graceful column.

On the second floor, in the all-white master bedroom, Mackintosh installed a barrel vault above the bed. For the mistress of the house, he designed a dressing table, a mirror, and chairs with ladder backs that are today considered classics. The refinement of this room's decor lies in its stripped-down geometric purity, combined with a moderate use of carefully chosen ornament. It is a far cry from the flowery transports of Art Nouveau, and the opposition between ornament and geometric severity, between white wall surfaces and dark wood, is characteristic of this new art of interior design.

In 1901 the design for the Hill House was entered into an international design competition for "an art lover's country house" organized by a German decorative arts magazine, and Mackintosh exhibited his furniture designs at the Vienna Secession. On that occasion, students carried him in triumph through the streets of Vienna. Mackintosh's design message would be taken up by all the members of the Vienna School, and the work of Josef Hoffmann and of Adolf Loos would owe everything to his example.

The music alcove in the drawing room.

Preceding page: The elegance and linear austerity of the entrance hall.

Opposite: The dining room, paneled in dark wood.

The fireplace in the drawing room is faced with multicolored mosaics.

*Opposite: Austere geometry for the lamps and wallpaper
of the drawing room.*

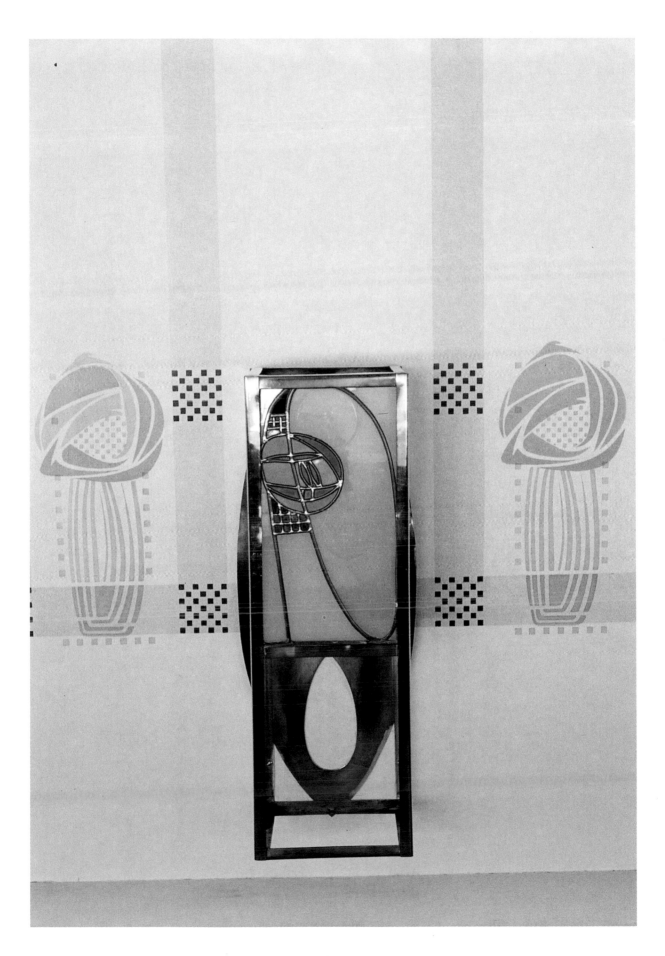

The luxury and simplicity of
the master bedroom.

The large, south-facing window bay in the drawing room;
the curtains are by Margaret Macdonald.

Opposite: Small squares and rosebuds in the mistress's dressing room.

MALLET HOUSE

VARENGEVILLE-SUR-MER

Architect
EDWIN LUTYENS

Sir Edwin Lutyens (1869–1944) was the great official architect of Great Britain at the start of the twentieth century. Knighted and showered with honors though he was, the major treatises on modern architecture have generally ignored or neglected his very real contribution. His body of work is enormous, as he designed more than three hundred buildings, ranging from cottages in the garden suburb of Hampstead, England, to the monumental viceroy's residence in India, which led in turn to his drawing up the city plan for New Delhi (1912).

He was quickly forgotten after his death, in part because he refused to follow the principles of the modern movement, as defined by its official theorist, Siegfried Giedion. It was not until the postmodern movement of the 1970s and the growing influence of such architects as American Robert Venturi that handsome and intelligent architecture was again allowed to use humor, make subtle allusions to the history of architecture, and put contradictory elements of composition into play.

If Lutyens has been restored to his rightful place it is for the relevance of his relation to the history of architecture. At a time when buildings were routinely stripped of all ornament and emptied of any symbolism, his work expressed a love of architectural composition, beautiful plans, and volumes, as well as an extraordinary feel for landscape.

Architects gifted with a sense for landscape, as Lutyens was, are very rare; all the great houses he built give the impression of having always existed on the same spot, although he designed them from the ground up, with the collaboration of landscape designer Gertrude Jekyll.

England may have been the world's leading industrial nation, but it energetically exalted the traditional values of home and family, and Lutyens's first projects were inspired by the very principles that guided the building of Philip Webb's Red House. One finds there the same integrity of structure, the same desire to create harmony between the building and its site, the same respect for the local culture and for using traditional construction methods with regional materials, and the same refusal to overuse ornament. The Arts and Crafts movement would dominate the decorative arts in England until 1914, flowering primarily in the English countryside.

Sir Edwin Lutyens was born in London in 1869, the same year as Frank Lloyd Wright, who would also create a very large number of residences. He was the eleventh in a family of fourteen children; his father, a captain in the army, retired from the service to become a painter of modest renown. At sixteen Edwin was sent off to study archi-

tecture at what became the Royal College of Art, and in 1887 he joined the London office of Ernest George and Harold Peto for two years. It was there that he met his friend Herbert Baker, with whom he would later collaborate on the city plan of New Delhi.

What particularly strikes Lutyens's biographers is his freedom of spirit within the framework of the schools and styles of the period. Lutyens opened his own architectural office in 1894 and over the next thirty years designed more than thirty large country houses. His abundant production offers a great wealth of solutions and variations on the theme of the country house, somewhat like the set of villas along the Brenta by Palladio or the collection of homes designed by Frank Lloyd Wright or Le Corbusier.

It was in 1897, through Mrs. Earle, an aunt of Lady Emily Lutyens, Sir Edwin's wife, that the Frenchman Guillaume Mallet (1860–1946) met the young architect, then twenty-eight and totally unknown. Mallet commissioned him to enlarge a building situated at the top of a thirty-acre park by adding an enormous music room, and to wholly redesign the park by creating a succession of gardens.

In front of the entrance façade, Lutyens and his longtime collaborator Gertrude Jekyll designed a series of open-air "rooms" along two axes: a north-south one leading from the street to the entrance, and an east-west one parallel to the façade of the house. The two axes converge at a circle in front of the main entrance.

While the garden in front of the house was designed as a series of enclosures offering limited views, the sea-facing side of the house overlooks the park with its luxurious vegetation. The house had been sited at the highest point of the property just to provide those sweeping, dream-inducing views—the ultimate goal of the setting. Lutyens and Jekyll took their cue from Italian architect Leon Battista Alberti, who held that the garden must be an extension of the house, expressed in a geometric design; they reintroduced a sense of unity between house and garden, between the architecture and surrounding landscape. Some picturesque elements punctuate the garden: a pergola, terraced walkways, geometrical plantings, arches of greenery, circles, alcoves, and so on. They were thus following in the tradition of the walled gardens of the Middle Ages, rectangular or square, in which gravel paths were overarched with arbors of wood or osier trained with roses, vines, or ivy; the purpose was to provide shaded walkways at a time when pale complexions were particularly sought after.

The park contains numerous species of trees: magnolias, bamboo, Chinese camellias, Himalayan rhododendrons, Japanese maples,

Opposite: Twinhood as a decorative theme
(west façade).

blue cedars from the Atlas Mountains, giant cypresses from Cyprus, azaleas from Turkey . . . This natural luxuriance is ordered and disciplined by a wise and knowing architecture: "Every garden design must have a structure, a central idea, which it beautifully expresses. Each wall, each path, each stone and flower must be in harmony with the central idea," wrote Lutyens. The Bois des Moutiers, as the site is now known, derives its charm from its "garden rooms," each of which contains its own plants and its own combination of colors. Here, nature and culture are one.

A DREAM HOUSE

This house is one of the rare examples of Arts and Crafts architecture in France, and the product of an entire tradition of English architectural and gardening know-how. Lutyens used the technique of successive additions to transform this Norman structure into an elegant English cottage: starting with the original rectangular floor plan he added architectural elements typical of Old England to each of the four façades. The entrance façade was endowed with a porch and a large, massive chimney; the two side façades were extended, on the west by twin gables, and on the east by the newly created music room; and a terrace overlooking the park was joined to the sea façade by a series of steps and a lovely covered walkway.

In this way Lutyens transformed an ordinary building into a sumptuous and typically English cottage, showing that the restoration of an old building can and must be genuinely creative work. The design he developed is based on a masterful use of asymmetry. The entrance porch and the oriel window of the music room, two projecting elements, are countered by the vertical thrust of the large chimney. On the sea side, the projecting wing of the new music room is joined to the original structure. Lutyens enjoyed using a diversity of architectural elements and setting them off against each other by a subtle play of their unequal masses.

It is here that the French school of perfectly classical composition diverges from the characteristically English school based on an aesthetic of the picturesque. In the place of French monumentalism, it offers a natural arrangement of masses. The Mallet House is not a simple house placed on the ground but a solid structure rooted to the land by its peripheral architectural parts, which follow the declivities of the site and perfectly relate the architecture to its setting. The massive effect of these volumes is accentuated by the small-paned window openings, placed high on the walls, or in the form of tall oriel windows.

The interior of the original structure was entirely reworked, as Lutyens established the music room on the first floor and extended the west wall to insert a service area and bathrooms on the second floor. All the areas of the house radiate out from the hall: the monumental staircase on the left, providing access to the bedrooms; the music room, on an axis with the entrance to the drawing room; and to the right, the service areas. The inside of the house is of oak: the walls, painted white, feature paneled oak wainscoting, and the doors are of solid oak, as is the furniture, which Lutyens designed himself.

A large staircase of natural oak leads to the bedrooms, each door of which is adorned with a multicolored plaster decoration by Robert Anning Bell: mermaids, butterflies, flowers, and female faces of Pre-Raphaelite inspiration. A tapestry designed by Burne-Jones depicting the Three Magi against a background of blue cedars hangs on one wall of the staircase, lit by three large vertical windows that bear a distinct resemblance to those Mackintosh designed in Glasgow.

The most majestic room in the house is the music room, designed by Lutyens to be two stories high to accommodate an organ in the upper gallery. The space is lit by an oriel window on either side opening onto the park. Virtual glass walls, they rise to the room's full height and have an accordionlike curvature to strengthen their wooden framing; Lutyens even designed handsome metal catches to open the windows' small panes. Two side recesses, lit by arched windows, provide access to the terrace.

At the other end of the music room Lutyens installed a small reading nook under a mezzanine, for which he provided light by means of windows set between heavy white stone uprights. The stone pillars that support this mezzanine end in strange capitals, also created by Lutyens, who had no compunction about distorting wood construction elements: beams, joists, railings. A large chimneypiece in the medieval style extends the full height of the room, accentuating the monumental elegance of this space, where an intimate reading corner can coexist with a vast area designed to resonate with music.

To create the handsome coffered ceiling, decorated with plaster floral designs, Lutyens called on his Arts and Crafts staffer Bankart. The walls of the music room are paneled in oak for acoustical purposes. This room is the house's center, where large gatherings were held; vast and simple, it is bare in the extreme, except for the reproduction of an Italian primitive.

The decorative strategy of large white walls accented with the color of natural oak is very much in the spirit of Mackintosh, Frank Lloyd Wright, or Viennese architect Josef Hoffmann.

The Mallet House is exceptional for the harmony it achieves between its architecture and the site, for its perfect equilibrium. We owe the preservation of this house to Mme Mary Mallet, who has taken responsibility for its upkeep since 1955. As she remarked, "Houses, gardens especially, are so ephemeral. . . . They'll disappear after we're gone, which is only right."

Opposite: Above the staircase hangs
a portrait of Pascaline Mallet.

The two-story-high music room, which opens onto the park.

The upper gallery in the music room.

A "garden room."

THE HOUSE OF VICTOR HORTA

BRUSSELS

The year 1893 marks the birth of the Art Nouveau movement. In London the design review the *Studio* began publication in that year, widely disseminating English ideas on the art of interior decoration; and in Brussels, using a radically new style, the architect Victor Horta built the Tassel House, the first private home conceived as a total work of art.

The city of Brussels, where Horta's talents would blossom, was a very rich artistic center. A cultural crossroads, it rivaled Paris in the visual and literary arts, even surpassing it to some extent, as the French capital was still under the heavy yoke of the Ecole des Beaux-Arts, the various academies, and the neoclassical style.

The symbolist and Impressionist movements were both recognized in Brussels long before they made their mark in Paris, and Brussels was also the uncontested capital of Art Nouveau, with Horta as its virtuoso. The most brilliant creation of Art Nouveau in Belgium was the Tassel House. The building marks the birth of the style, which would soon be relayed throughout Europe by one project after another.

In the years when Art Nouveau was taking hold, Brussels was enjoying a population and construction boom. More than 1,500 Art Nouveau buildings went up between 1890 and 1914, accounting for more than 5 percent of total construction. Both the progressive middle class and the artistic avant-garde embraced the style; and a multitude of artisans—glassworkers, mosaicists, painters, carpenters, metalworkers, and cabinetmakers—broke ranks with neoclassicism to join the new school of architecture. The English Arts and Crafts movement was a crucial influence, William Morris being well known thanks to Belgian architect Gustave Serrurier Bovy, who imported Morris's textiles and other handicrafts from England.

The massive industrial production of objects belonging to an ossified aesthetic drove European artists as a group to redefine their own aesthetic in terms of a new formal unity and a new relation between spatial structure, ornament, and furniture. The return to first principles forced them to redesign absolutely everything, from house plans to textile designs, furniture, door handles, flooring, lamps, and other common objects, in an attempt to avoid the commercial vulgarity William Morris had predicted would be the ultimate consequence of mechanical production.

VICTOR HORTA (1861–1947)

Victor Horta was born in Ghent in 1861. At the age of seventeen, against the will of his father, a carpenter, he left for Paris, where

Architect
VICTOR HORTA

he entered the atelier of the architect and decorator Jules Debuysson. "My stay in Paris, the walks I took, and the visits to monuments and museums opened all the doors in my artist's heart. No other school could have instilled in me greater enthusiasm for architecture than the sight and study of the monuments of Paris, which made a lasting impression on me," wrote Horta in his memoirs.

In 1880, after the death of his father, Horta returned to Belgium and enrolled in the Académie des Beaux-Arts in Brussels. He studied with Alphonse Balat (1818–1895), a neoclassical architect and favorite of Leopold II, designer of the Museum of Ancient Art in Brussels and most notably of the royal greenhouses in Laeken. As Horta wrote, "Balat was a superior man, a complete artist. . . . His works are masterpieces of their kind, yet he never dared to abandon traditional forms. Only when he came to use iron, a material the Greeks had never used in building, was he able to follow his personal inspiration and create an admirable work: the Laeken greenhouses. Seeing the flight of this powerful intelligence hampered by the memory of forms from the past, except in unusual cases such as the greenhouses, I felt a revolt stirring in me and resolved to try something else: to give life, loyally and sincerely, to the forms that welled up in my imagination" (*L'Energie belge*, 1906).

Horta won a number of competitions and prizes before launching his own firm in 1885 with the purpose of building three houses in Ghent. In 1889 he returned to Paris for the Exposition Universelle, where the Eiffel Tower and the Machine Gallery were the two masterpieces of metal construction, then all the rage. It was there that the infinite possibilities of metal were revealed to him.

HORTA AND VIOLLET-LE-DUC

The figure who most influenced Horta during his formative years was the great nineteenth-century theorist of architecture Eugène Emmanuel Viollet-le-Duc. His impact on the rationalist movement of the end of the century was considerable. Viollet-le-Duc attacked the academicist education provided by the Ecole des Beaux-Arts, which enslaved architects to historical forms, and Horta agreed with Viollet-le-Duc's refusal to use the architectural forms of the past. A new vocabulary needed to be developed, one made possible by the use of iron and cast iron in construction and by the application of rational methods: "Be true to the plan, true to the process of construction. Being true to the plan lies in fulfilling exactly, scrupulously, the conditions set by specific requirements. Being true to the processes of construction lies in

Opposite: House and studio at 23–25, rue Américaine in the Saint-Gilles quarter of Brussels.

using materials in accordance with their qualities and properties" (*Entretiens sur l'architecture [Discourses on Architecture]*, 1858–72). From his earliest projects, Horta would follow Viollet-le-Duc's precepts to the letter, eventually going beyond them to create a style in which structure and ornament were intimately linked.

HORTA'S HOUSE, 1898

When Horta decided to build his own house, he was thirty-seven years old and had already completed his major works: the Tassel House (1893), the Solvay House (1894), and the Maison du Peuple (1895). Successful in his career, assured of a regular influx of commissions, Horta could now afford to think of applying the inventions and solutions developed in constructing others' houses to his own.

He bought two adjacent lots at 25, rue Américaine, in the Saint-Gilles quarter of Brussels. He would build his house on one and his architecture studio on the other, preferring two adjoining buildings to a structure that was all of one piece. He created slight differences in the two façades, the residence having four floors and the studio three; each has its own entrance.

The studio's façade is the more open to the street: a large window adorned with two slender cast-iron columns allows light into the offices on the ground floor. On the second floor, Horta lit the studio's waiting room with a double bay supported by a square, centrally placed cast-iron column. Wooden frames for three bays are set within this double arch. On the third floor, the large designers' studio is illuminated by a veritable wall of glass, with two cast-iron columns supporting the lintel, above which is a small cornice. The only ornamentation on this façade is the swelling of stone that supports the central window column on the second floor, and the two small openings for water runoff.

The façade of the residence appears more slender because of its additional floor. A stone oriel window on the third floor signals Horta's drawing room. Beneath this traditional element of Brussels domestic architecture, a balcony is suspended from three slender metal brackets. The glass flooring of the balcony serves as an awning to protect the house's entrance.

Horta has willfully defied the laws of statics by placing the heavier elements at the top and the lighter ones closer to the ground. In this way he manages to produce an effect of elevation crowned by a wrought-iron guardrail in the shape of two graceful dragonfly wings. These façades may not be spectacular in terms of their plasticity, but they hold interest for the great care taken in the design of every detail, every articulation between iron and stone, and each transition between the columnlike suspending elements and brackets.

The staircase is the heart of the house. Here Horta was faithful to the principles he had evolved in building other homes, and he used the stair as a well of interior light, as the element linking all of the spaces in the house. What strikes the visitor who enters for the first time is the contrast of colors: the white Carrara marble veined with gray, the lower portion of the walls marked with orange bands. The surprise effect is considerable, as the somewhat sober stone exteriors give no indication of the interior well of light; from nowhere on the outside is the grand staircase visible. It is one of the most lovely entrances to a house anywhere—modest in scale, but luxurious in its architectural treatment of the materials. Horta manages to achieve a fascinating harmony between the light cascading down from the skylights above and its reflection off the warm and cold hues of wood and marble.

Reaching the top floor of the house, one is dazzled by the luminous vault of glass: it is the house's moment of truth, its act of bravura, and the place that gives sense to its spatial structure. Horta reduced the size of the stairs as they rise, in order for the light to flood all the floors and for the orange tint, reflected to eternity in two mirrors shaped like butterfly wings, to spread throughout. The fine metal grillwork, the swirling handrails of carved red wood, and the golden arabesques supporting them induce a sensation of dizziness. "The sun is the house's true host": this is the astonishing mastery of the glass vault, which, like a chord on the organ, makes all the spaces in the house vibrate in unison. Horta has managed to create an introverted world made up of light and warm colors.

Victor Horta avoids any reference to the history of architecture and its styles, turning instead toward nature. The growth of plants was to figure even in the structure of his buildings: the heavy and imposing masses of traditional European architecture vanish to make room for transparent spaces where light again moves freely, as in the rococo interiors of the eighteenth century. Horta drew from nature to produce decorative elements in plaster, cast iron, carved wood, and undulating mosaics, even managing to turn marble into sinuous, multicolored forms. Glass becomes as light as a flower or a dragonfly's wing, metal structures twine like tendrils, and the carved wood of the furniture assumes a surprising plasticity.

From his observation of industrial construction (steel bridges, greenhouses, and so forth), in which natural light floods in through large glassed surfaces, Horta would make the glass expanse his particular theme, rendering it in a multitude of forms, including vaults, cupolas (either orthogonal or circular), and freeform shapes.

All this was made possible by his exceptional clients—Armand Solvay, Tassel, Edmond van Eetvelde—who were enlightened businessmen with a perfect understanding of the conditions needed to realize new commissions. The new era called for new men and a new art—Art Nouveau. The cultural and artistic dynamism of the final years of the nineteenth century is arresting, the symbol we associate with that time being spaces where air and light express the pervading social dynamism.

Horta's stay in the United States, from 1914 to 1919, would bring him into contact with a new form of the modern, one in which straight lines prevailed, but it was Horta who restored to architecture a freedom of composition that academicism had stifled.

*Opposite: The staircase,
as seen from the music room.*

The glass vault floods the center of the house with light.

Opposite: The music room.

The dining room.

Multicolored mosaics and marble.

Opposite: The music room—marble column and arabesque.

In a bedroom, lamps have been transformed into flowers.

*Opposite: A design for a glass pavilion that was
never executed hangs in the studio.*

THE GÜELL PALACE

BARCELONA

At his death on June 12, 1926, the great Catalan architect Antonio Gaudí y Cornet (1852–1926) was carried in state from the Santa Cruz hospital in old Barcelona to the church of the Sagrada Familia. As the slow funeral procession wound through the streets, thousands of Barcelonans joined step to pay their last respects to this most Catalan of Catalan artists. Gaudí had become a popular hero, and the government had ordered his burial in the crypt of the still unfinished church, to which the Pope consented. Thus the architect's body rests at the heart of the great site where he had worked for more than forty years.

Antonio Gaudí was born in Reus, near Tarragona, Spain, in 1852, the son of Francisco Gaudí, a tinsmith. After completing secondary school in Reus, Gaudí entered the Barcelona School of Architecture in 1870, where he earned his degree in 1878. He then worked for five years with the architect Josep Fontseré, assisting with various projects in Barcelona's Parque de la Ciutadella. The gates and certain details of the elaborate Cascade are attributed to him. He also won a competition organized by the city of Barcelona for the design of a street lamp, two of which can still be seen on the Plaza Real. Then, in 1883, he designed his first house, a summer home for Manuel Vicens i Montaner, a ceramic tile manufacturer.

Gaudí's attraction to Eastern architecture can already be felt in this project, which features the rich decorations, turrets, and numerous recesses that were to become more and more prevalent in his work. Gaudí studied Eastern architecture attentively in the rich collection of photographs belonging to the Barcelona School of Architecture. Looking carefully at his works, one recognizes motifs from Indian architecture, and the influence of Mozarabic architecture on Catalan is today quite obvious. The Alcazar in Seville, the mosque in Córdoba, and the Alhambra in Granada are all nearby; those monumental constructions, the intact vestiges of Islamic Spain, were the source of the Catalan master's dreams.

In the Casa Vicens, beyond the very strong Mudejar influence, one discovers the highly personal style of a master of Art Nouveau. Already, Gaudí was making openings in the shape of parabolic arches and immoderately mixing polychrome ceramics with stone and dark red brick. At the top of the house he designed massive brick corbels to support openwork galleries. The roof, ringed by a circular walkway, is decorated with polychrome tiles and punctuated with cupolas. And Gaudí designed fantastical wrought-iron gates, whose intricate traceries echo the exotic flora of the garden.

Behind the Sobrellans Palace, built by Joan Martorell for the marquis of Comillas,

Architect
ANTONIO GAUDÍ

construction proceeded from 1883 to 1885 on a villa for Máximo Diáz de Quijano, the marquis's brother-in-law. Gaudí designed the villa's tower, facing it with tiles in the Moorish style, and decorated the interior with handsome wooden ceilings inlaid with white marble.

In 1883 Gaudí received his first commission from his friend and patron Eusebi Güell to build a hunting lodge near Sitges. The wealthy industrialist would eventually commission more than a hundred projects from Gaudí. In that year, Güell had bought a farm called Can Cayas de la Riera, near Can Feliu, his estate in Las Corts de Sarriá. Güell charged Gaudí with building the gates and gatehouses and renovating the house and garden. Gaudí designed extremely beautiful stables, capped by a succession of parabolic arches made of brick and coated with a white finish. He also designed a riding hall surmounted by a white cupola, brightened at its center by a heavy turret decorated with a mosaic of ceramic fragments. This decorative technique, which he would return to often, was first used for the Güell farm. Its decorative elegance aside, the project presents new structural solutions, as it is also the first time Gaudí used parabolic arcades visible from both inside and outside the building.

The year 1883, when he was thirty-one years old, was a very good one for Gaudí, as he was chosen also by the Asociación Espiritual de Devotos de San José to construct a church in honor of the Holy Family. Initially this project had been given to the architect Paulo del Villar, in whose studio Gaudí had worked as a student, but in 1883 the commission was taken away from Villar on the recommendation of Joan Martorell, with whom Gaudí was working closely on a study of the Gothic style. It was with this style in mind that Gaudí invented an entirely personal vision of the monumental.

In 1895 the Asociación received a very large gift, which it was anxious to use quickly, and Gaudí was forced to revise the project and conceive it on a monumental scale. As a result, the church evolved into a veritable cathedral, but when the funds dried up, it was fated to remain in an unfinished state. The Sagrada Familia would haunt Gaudí for the rest of his life. In 1886 he believed the work could be completed within ten years, provided he were granted the sum of 360,000 pesetas annually. But because the church had been conceived as an expiatory church, it could be built only with funds deriving from gifts or charity. The work came to a halt with World War I, leaving a forest of steeples in an irregular circle, topped by porcelain-studded pinnacles; the main façade is a hundred meters high, but there is nothing behind it. Gaudí set up his workshop in the middle of the site and,

Opposite: Decorative chimneys dot the roof terrace.

with the help of numerous plaster models, directed the many artisans, including bricklayers, stonecutters, carpenters, sculptors, and ceramists. This huge commission did not monopolize Gaudí's career, however; in addition he built numerous other structures, from the Bishop's Palace in Astorga to the College of Santa Teresa de Jesús, as well as many private residences.

THE GÜELL PALACE (1885–89)

Eusebi Güell i Bacigolupi was a modern Catalan industrialist who made his fortune in the textile industry. He traveled extensively, particularly to Great Britain, where he was exposed to the artistic currents of the Arts and Crafts movement. Gaudí was invited into Güell's home, the site of grand receptions that were attended by large numbers of artists, and where the works of the Pre-Raphaelite poet Dante Gabriel Rossetti were read and the innovative ideas of William Morris and John Ruskin discussed.

Güell bought a plot of land of 49 feet (15 meters) deep by 72 feet (22 meters) wide in the Calle Conde del Asalto, today renamed Calle Nou de la Rambla. The Güell family already owned a house on the Ramblas and two others on the site where the new palace stands today; the hallway connecting the two houses still exists. Güell wanted a new structure large enough to house his library and collection of antiquities and permit the expansion of his rich social life.

To solve the problem presented by the narrow plot, Gaudí arranged the six levels of the palace around an interior court. The stables are located in the basement; the main drawing room and reception areas, on the second floor. The two top floors were reserved for the private activities of daily life, and the sixth level corresponds to the roof terrace.

The structure of the building is of Mediterranean and Arabic inspiration. The palace is closed to the street, and all the rooms are arranged around the large empty center, surmounted by a parabolic cupola. The court was used for receptions and musical concerts, as well as for dances and other festivities.

The underground stables are among the most original features of the Güell Palace. Two ramps lead down to them, one spiraling around one of the enormous brick pillars that support the massive structure. Gaudí installed an elaborate ventilation system to keep odors from penetrating to the upper floors. A set of flattened cupolas transmits the weight to large round and square pillars topped by brick capitals.

In addition to brick, Gaudí used iron for the structure of the service staircase, which provides access to all the floors. On the ground floor, a large lobby was created to accommodate carriages entering through the wrought-iron gates of the severe street façade. Thus in

spite of the narrow plot the architect managed to suspend the palace above ground, freeing space to welcome guests with great ceremony. A grand staircase leads through the mezzanine to the second floor, where, at the core of the palace, the dazzled visitor discovers a vast hall that resembles a Baroque church. Its cupola is inset with numerous glass bricks and soars more than 65 feet (20 meters) above the ground. It rests on four parabolic vaults, which diffuse a soft light through a network of wrought-iron trellises and grills.

In the design and appointment of the interior spaces, Gaudí proved to be an enlightened director of social life. For Güell, a music lover, the architect designed an organ, placing the pipes in an upper gallery to give the instrument a wonderful resonance. In the great hall, around which the life of the palace revolved, an altar was installed. The living room is located toward the back of the lot; its beech coffered ceiling is supported by slender columns, and daylight enters through a succession of elliptical arches. Above the library, a small hanging garden was created. The drawing rooms overlooking the Calle Nou de la Rambla have coffered ceilings of eucalyptus and cypress ornamented with gilded and twisted metal elements. The great richness of these decorations serves a structural purpose as well, since they support the bedrooms and bathrooms of the floor above. For closing off the balconies, Gaudí designed metallic shutters that filter daylight while allowing air to circulate. The top floor of the palace was reserved for the servant quarters, and above it is the roof terrace, where the architect planted his colorful pinnacles. While most architects leave roofs to the pigeons, Gaudí decided to create a spectacular and joyous roofscape composed of more than eighteen chimneys and ventilation towers in a multitude of shapes and colorful materials, a theme he was to pursue both in the Casa Batlló and the Casa Milá. Picasso, whose studio was across the street, could observe these structures whenever he came or went.

The Güell Palace is Gaudí's first great baroque manifesto, mingling all the influences of Gothic and, especially, Muslim and Indian architecture. His unbridled taste for decorative excess, exotic woods, stone, brick, twisted metal, and trellises make Gaudí the true descendant of the master builders of Islamic Spain, who scattered religious structures and luxurious residential complexes all over the country. No one was better able than Gaudí to understand the Moorish tradition, yet few historians have pointed to this crucial affiliation of the Catalan master.

On June 12, 1926, Gaudí was knocked down by a streetcar at the corner of the Gran Via de Las Corts and Calle Bailen. Gravely injured, he was taken to a modest hospital in Santa Creu. When his friends offered to move him to a private clinic, Gaudí refused, saying, "My place is here among the poor."

A wrought-iron balcony on the street façade.

Stone capitals decorated with wrought iron.

Opposite: Screen and staircase on the mezzanine.

The dining room is decorated with carved-wood paneling and wrought iron.

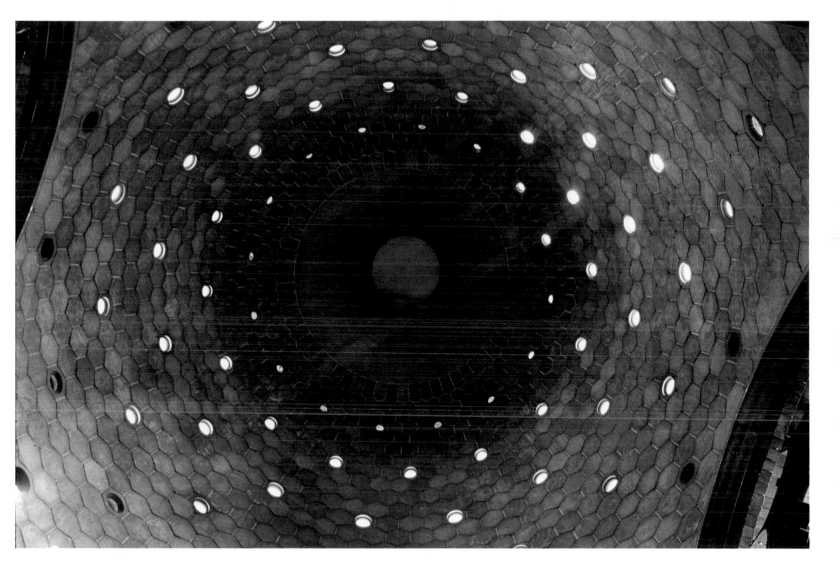

The cupola of the great hall is inset with glass bricks.

*A parabolic arch and wall sconce
in the great hall.*

Parabolic arches front the windows.

Opposite: The coffered wood and wrought-iron ceiling in the drawing room.

THE HOUSE OF PIERRE LOTI

ROCHEFORT

Pierre Loti's house is a magical place that takes you to the four corners of the earth and on a voyage through time, all within the confines of a gray port city whose streets are laid out on a grid devoid of the slightest trace of fantasy. In the house Loti shows a masterful handling of scenic effects, using light, materials, emotional contrasts, and the infinite art of passages and transitions with consummate skill. At the same time that he preserved his childhood home, Loti invented a variety of spaces that faithfully re-create the places he had traveled to and used as the settings for his most successful novels.

Julien Viaud, known as Pierre Loti (1850–1923), was born into a Protestant family in Rochefort at no. 141 on the street that today bears his name. His father, Théodore Viaud, was secretary in chief of the Protestant mission at Rochefort. A self-taught man, in his spare time he wrote a *History of the Town and Port of Rochefort*; he was also an enthusiastic amateur painter of portraits and landscapes. Loti's mother, Nadine Texier, was born in Rochefort in 1810, in her family's house at no. 141; she married Théodore, who lived across the street, in 1830. Julien was born twenty years later, on January 14, 1850, and, being the last of three children, was inevitably overprotected. His older brother, Gustave (1838–1865), a navy doctor who sailed for Tahiti in 1860 and sent regular letters back to his younger brother, would become Julien's role model and a decisive influence on his fate. From the enchanted islands of Tahiti he brought back seashells, and dreams of these distant countries began to stir the child's rich imagination.

After his graduation from the Naval Academy, Julien traveled widely and kept a record of his many voyages, interspersing his writing with sketches. In May 1877, following the assassination of the French and German consuls in Thessalonika, which at the time belonged to Turkey, the French fleet in the Mediterranean was dispatched to the Middle East. Julien discovered Constantinople: he rented a house in the old quarter of Eyoub, adopted Turkish dress, and rapidly melded into the Muslim population. There he would fall in love, and out of the experience came his first Oriental novel, *Aziyadé*, published in 1879. On February 24, 1881, at Golfe-Juan, he received official promotion to the rank of lieutenant first class. His family's debts could now gradually be paid off, and his royalties as an author would allow him to transform the family house.

PIERRE LOTI

into the whitewashed walls of the Rochefort house the highly colored settings that had so deeply penetrated his memory. In 1876 Pierre Loti became his own architect and started the slow transformation, which proceeded in two stages: from 1876 to 1895 in the original building at no. 141, and from 1895 on in the adjoining building at no. 139, which Loti bought, doubling the size of his imaginary museum. Pierre Loti's first creation, realized in 1877 while he was writing *Aziyadé*, was the Turkish Room on the third floor of the original house. The Arabian Room, also on the third floor, appeared next, in 1884, the year he published *Les Trois Dames de la Kasbah*. In 1886, on his return from the China campaign, Loti created the Japanese pagoda with the help of 1,200 pounds of baggage brought back from the Orient; *Madame Chrysanthème* and *Japoneries d'automne* were published in 1887 and 1889, respectively. In 1887–88 the Gothic Room replaced his sister Marie's old painting studio. And in 1895, once he had acquired the neighboring building, Loti was able to develop his imaginary museum around the Renaissance Room, his most monumental creation; that same year he installed the mosque on the floor above. In 1902 he put the finishing touches on his composition with the creation of the Chinese Room, using furnishings brought back from the Imperial Palace in Peking, at the same time publishing *Les Derniers Jours de Pékin*.

THE RED AND BLUE DRAWING ROOMS

After crossing a small vestibule, one enters two plush drawing rooms that give no hint of the fantasies still ahead. Orderly and conventional, the first served the Viaud family as a place in which to rest and gather in the evenings. Pierre Loti did not preserve the red drawing room's original state, however. He replaced the old, faded wallpaper with purple velvet, on which he hung a gallery of portraits: his mother, his sister Marie, his niece Ninette, and two likenesses of himself—the principal actor in the play about to unfold—both by the Swiss painter Edmond de Pury, one showing him as a Saracen chief and the other as a naval officer.

The blue drawing room was created in the adjoining house. Dubbed the Louis XVI Salon, it was the favorite room of Pierre Loti's wife, Blanche. We are now, as it were, in the foyer of the theater, where gilt, moldings, rugs, gauze curtains, and a glass chandelier prepare us for a transition.

THE ROCHEFORT HOUSE

As he transcribed his stories onto paper, Loti felt a corresponding urge to build and to etch

Opposite: The unprepossessing façade of 141, rue Pierre-Loti, in Rochefort.

THE RENAISSANCE ROOM

Lifting aside the heavy drapery, one finds oneself in the largest room of the house and the most monumental for its height and disproportionate size: we have entered a Renaissance château. The two comfortably furnished drawing rooms are intimate in scale, but here Loti seeks to surprise us, to stagger us with the grandeur of the room's proportions. A grand staircase, flanked by two stone lions, makes its majestic ascent, and a massive fireplace rises to the room's full height. The space is decorated with tapestries, chests, and candelabras; heavy wooden beams support the coffered ceiling. A floor was removed to create the necessary height, and a gallery was installed, access to which is gained by a spiral staircase leading to the rooms on the second floor.

In 1902, in order to create a new Chinese Room, Loti had a small courtyard next to the Renaissance Room covered over. The room no longer exists, but it was there that, in 1903, he held a Chinese celebration, attended by more than two hundred guests dressed in period costumes.

THE GOTHIC ROOM

In 1888 Loti transformed the former painting studio of his sister Marie into the Gothic Room. He bought two sets of authentic ogival arches for it in nearby Marennes and placed them against the west wall, facing a large fireplace of carved walnut. The floor is covered with wide planks of solid wood, and the ceiling beams are decorated with white chevrons.

To inaugurate the room in 1888, he held his first party, a magical transposition to the Middle Ages. Thirty or so guests gathered in princely costumes and suits of armor, the master of the house was surrounded by his pages, and the menu for the gargantuan feast featured every culinary specialty of the medieval period. A fascination with the Middle Ages was characteristic of the Romantic movement, which rediscovered the period along with the Renaissance in the wake of Prosper Mérimée and Eugène Emmanuel Viollet-le-Duc—who went so far as to rebuild Pierrefonds Castle and the fortress of Carcassonne.

THE MOSQUE

Reached by the monumental staircase of the Renaissance Room, the mosque was built by Loti in 1896. Its white walls are covered with Oriental ceramic tiles, five Moorish arches rest on slender columns of pink marble, and the whole is lit by small French windows. It is a real mosque, partially reconstructed from materials Loti bought in 1894 on his voyage to Syria: "I made it out of the tiles of a mosque in Damascus that was being destroyed, and all rubble of which I bought for 15,000 francs, not a penny more." To this magnificent site Loti transferred Aziyadé's stela, leaving the Topkapi cemetery with an exact copy. Almond green in color, it is crowned by a flowering basket, a characteristic sign of Turkish women's tombs.

THE TURKISH ROOM

In November 1877 Loti began converting his Aunt Lalie's old room: "I furnished it more or less in the Turkish manner with cushions of Asian silk and the knickknacks that the fire at my house in Eyoub and the Jewish moneylenders left me. It does bring to mind distantly the little drawing room draped in blue satin and scented with rose water that I had there, at the end of the Golden Horn." The ceiling is inspired by that of the Alhambra in Granada, which he had visited during a stopover in Malaga in 1869. The Turkish Room was redecorated several times, and it was there, at the end of the room, that Loti had himself photographed as an Arab warrior, surrounded by his Oriental hangings and multicolored woolen carpets.

THE ARABIAN ROOM

In 1884, the same year he published *Les Trois Dames de la Kasbah,* Loti completed the renovation of the Arabian Room on the third floor. The walls of this modest-sized room were hung with wool fabrics of reddish hues bearing geometric patterns similar to the patterns on the Oriental carpets covering the floor. Above these sumptuous Oriental materials rises a series of windowless arches made of plaster and inset with ancient ceramic tiles from the casbah in Algiers. Next to the entry door is an authentic Arabian stela, on which daylight falls vertically from above, reinforcing the dramatic effect that the director of this scene sought to create.

PIERRE LOTI'S BEDROOM

The visit ends here, in a room that reveals the author's absolute lucidity: its whitewashed walls, bare and monastic, are in complete contrast to the luxurious decorativeness elsewhere. It is furnished with an iron bed, narrow as a ship's bunk. Hung simply on the walls are an officer's sword, a fencing foil, and a revolver. A crucifix and a religious image stand as reminders of the Christian faith Loti had lost—the only religion embraced by this refined aesthete was the cult of beauty in beings and in things.

The house is fascinating for the interplay between architecture and fiction; the construction of these set pieces and the writing of the novels overlapped closely. Loti organized the house as a series of independent chapters that comprise a sampling of all the tastes of the second half of the nineteenth century: Orientalism, certainly, but also a passion for the Middle Ages, the Renaissance, and even the eighteenth century, which held such great significance for the Goncourt brothers. Pierre Loti liked to mix traditions, and in that he followed the predilection of his eclectic age. The house holds a valuable place in the history of art, along with other famous homes, such as the duc d'Aumale's in Chantilly and Victor Hugo's in Guernsey.

What makes this house so unusual is the lightning path it strikes through history and geography, spanning several centuries and darting across several continents. Loti summons up the history of art in each of his rooms and has an enormous capacity for wonder; re-creating settings was absolutely necessary for him to conduct his work. Known as the Enchanter, and universally famous, Loti died on June 5, 1923, partially crippled by paralysis. The house in Rochefort was given to the city and opened to the public in 1969.

The blue drawing room.

Preceding page: The secret garden.

The Renaissance Room.

The mosque with its Moorish arches.

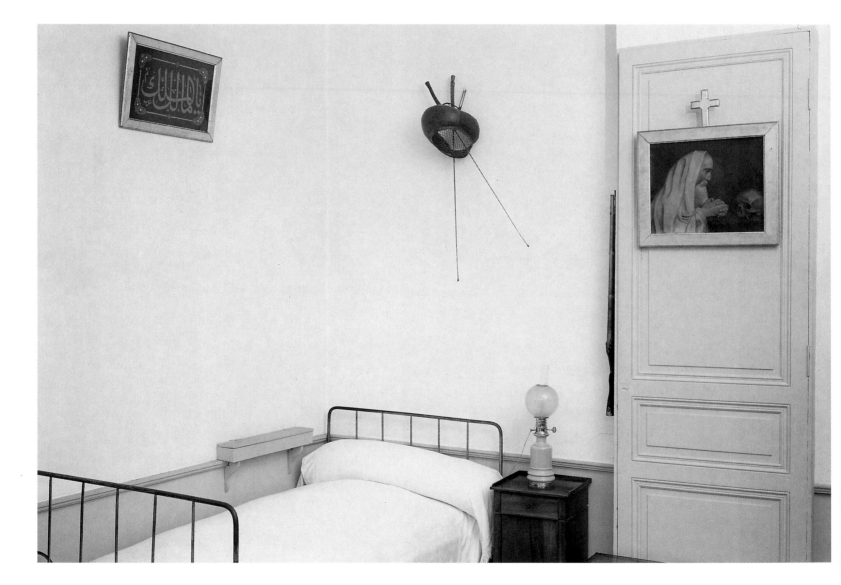

Loti's bare and monkish bedroom.

Opposite: The Gothic Room.

The mosque: catafalques and marble columns.

The landing leading to Pierre Loti's bedroom.

The Gothic Room with its ogival arches.

Opposite: The luxurious Turkish Room, renovated in 1877.

VILLA KERYLOS

BEAULIEU-SUR-MER

Theodore Reinach is the man truly responsible for the Villa Kerylos, a masterpiece of architectural reconstruction. One of the great Hellenists of his day, his dream was to build a villa that embodied the principles of classical Greek architecture. To do this, he chose a young Prix de Rome architect, Emmanuel Pontremoli. The project was financed by Reinach's personal fortune, which must have been considerable; the villa cost nine million gold francs in the currency of the time. Archaeological reconstruction projects were not unusual in the history of architecture: from 1846 on, the French government had provided grants for such scholars as Charles Garnier to travel to Athens and study its ancient monuments. Commissioning dozens of highly qualified designer-craftsmen in many fields, Reinach proved that only artists who are steeped in history can realize a masterpiece. It would be wrong to think of the Villa Kerylos merely as a rich man's folly; it is rather the expression of a learned man's culture, pushed to its utmost limit.

THEODORE REINACH

THE GOLDEN AGE OF THE PRIX DE ROME

Emmanuel Pontremoli (1865–1956) was thirty-seven years old when he was commissioned to make this faithful reconstruction of a classical Greek villa. A product of the Ecole des Beaux-Arts, he won the Prix de Rome and then was assigned to an archaeological dig restoring the great temple of Apollo at Didymus. Freshly returned to Paris, he was assisting in the renovation of the Rubens Gallery at the Louvre when he met Theodore Reinach.

He devoted himself exclusively to the Villa Kerylos from 1902 to 1908. Reinach perhaps chose him for the project in part because he was a native of Nice and understood the Mediterranean coast; Reinach was also struck by the young man's love of painting and his use of color in his designs. The deciding factor, however, was in all likelihood Pontremoli's faithful reconstruction of Pergamon, a site the architect found particularly fascinating because the Ionic order was dominant there, as can be seen in the powerful, tormented bas-reliefs on the great Altar of Zeus, which belongs to the same tradition as the Acropolis in Athens. This is not the classical antiquity of stiff and frozen statues. Pergamon is the site above all others where sculptural and architectural decoration is made to express life and movement, and where painting, also shed of its archaic origins, represents the figure in motion. The Villa Kerylos was therefore very much at the center of the new currents in architecture and city planning at the Ecole des Beaux-Arts in Paris.

The Villa Kerylos sits on the tip of a rocky

peninsula overlooking the sea between Fourmis Bay and the bay of Beaulieu-sur-Mer. The site was picked by Pontremoli himself for its resemblance to a Greek landscape: a spit of land fronting the Mediterranean. "The house," he wrote, "had to be incorporated into this stretch of coast from Nice to La Tourbie, fashioned on this tiny point, built to withstand the wind and bathe in sea and sun; at the same time, the site's natural beauty could in no way be diminished, and none of the trees so tenaciously clinging to the rocks could be destroyed."

The long shape of the rocky spur determined the elongated plan of the house and obliged the architect to construct it on several levels. Structures were built only on the east and south sides of the peristyle, leaving the area to the west free for a garden. Pontremoli placed the main rooms facing the sea: first, a low wing for guests; then, surrounding the peristyle and protecting it, the east and south wings, each two stories high. A three-story tower connects the two wings. A set of terraces, one of which opens onto the pergola, completes the complex. The garden is extremely simple, planted with knotty pines, cypresses, and succulents, the only luxuries being the sea and the light.

On entering, one finds the brilliant light and sunshine sharply contrasted by the cool and quiet of the peristyle. After the dazzling light, the eye adjusts slowly to being plunged in shade and discovers only gradually the columns and the frescoes, the colored flooring, and the precious objects: "Order is imposed by the correct proportions of the Ionic columns in the second tier and the Doric columns in the first," Pontremoli explains. "It is their rhythm and their dimensions that determine the scale of the house; all the rooms are governed by these proportions. The general rhythm creates an effect of harmony regardless of the colors or materials used. One must check the actual dimensions to realize that the house is quite small."

To execute the many facets of his decorative scheme, Pontremoli called on a large number of artist-craftsmen. The frescoes were faithfully re-created by the painter Karbowski, a student of Pierre-Cécile Puvis de Chavannes, in collaboration with Jaulmes; the stucco work was executed by Gasq; the vases and jars were the work of Lenoble; the marble was brought from Carrara by Nicoli; the architect's furniture designs were scrupulously followed by Bettenfeld and his cabinetmakers; the precious fabrics were reproduced by Ecochard; the fountains and the oil lamps by Yung.

In 1908 Theodore Reinach would take possession of the finished house, christening it with a name that could be pronounced as easily in Greek as in French, Kerylos.

Opposite: A Greek villa facing the Mediterranean.

THE PERISTYLE

The rooms of the house are arranged around the peristyle, an empty space that gives the whole its significance. Daylight enters in between its twelve monolithic Doric columns of white Carrara marble. The courtyard is paved in white marble; at its center is a delicate fountain shaded by an oleander that was left in place when construction began. As the only natural element in the space, the tree introduces a subtle asymmetry. In counterpoint to the immaculate whiteness of the marble, the walls are covered with delicate frescoes, executed according to the classical method of mixing encaustic and ground marble and applying them to fresh mortar. Pontremoli has attained a perfect balance between the massiveness of the Doric columns and the lightness of the frescoes that unfold as the visitor walks by.

The doors of the library and the *amphythyron* open onto the east side of the peristyle; facing them on the wall to the west are two niches containing statues of Homer and Hippocrates.

THE LIBRARY

In accordance with the precepts of Vitruvius, the library faces east to catch the morning sun and protect the books from the damp south and west winds, which could cause mildew. Scrolls are enclosed in cabinets embedded in the masonry, as in the ancient villa in Herculaneum where more than 1,800 papyrus scrolls, charred by lava, were found in 1762. Together with the *andron*, or drawing room, the library is the most sizable space in the house; it is illuminated by three large windows, which open onto a terrace facing the sea. The room is a story-and-a-half high because of a gallery built into the upper part of the west wall. Also worthy of note are the two large classical-style inlaid-oak tables at either end of the room; these three-footed tables were designed by Reinach himself. The visitor is struck by the extraordinary richness of the decor, the accuracy and completeness of the reconstruction, and the refinement accorded every detail.

THE TRICLINIUM

After crossing the *amphythyron*, the traditional Greek anteroom that leads into the public rooms and private apartments, one reaches the triclinium, or dining room, so called because of the three couches disposed around the dining table, the fourth side being left open for service. According to Vitruvius, a rich house might have several rooms of this kind: one facing north for summer use, and another facing west for the autumn. Tall French windows opening onto the garden offered guests a view of its vines, pergolas, and fountains. The Greeks ate their meals reclining on couches arranged around low tables; when men gathered to eat, as in the meal described by Plato in the *Symposium*, the master of the house would assign the guests their places, and the men would lie down on the couches side by side, leaning on their left elbows and eating with their fingers, using utensils only for liquid foods. In Pompeii, archaeologists have discovered massive stone couches, slightly sloping, which would have been covered with rugs and cushions. The triclinium at the Villa Kerylos preserves the classical layout. Set at right angles in the middle of the room, the couches have three legs and are made of inlaid wood. Theodore Reinach and his guests would take their places there, having first purified themselves and put on the chlamys, a short mantle worn by men in ancient Greece. The food was served in dishes made especially for the Villa Kerylos.

THE ANDRON

From the triclinium, one proceeds to the *andron* (drawing room), where three large bays ornamented with heavy bronze grills open onto the peristyle. The *andron* was reserved for gatherings of men. Vitruvius informs us that the rooms in a Greek house were situated in such a way that the women in the *gynaecium* and the men in the *andron* could live in total independence. The *andron* has more light than any other room in the house: Pontremoli chose white mosaics to reflect light onto the richly colored marble walls, which are inlaid with lines of white stucco. The room's importance is underscored by the presence at its west end of a domestic altar of white Carrara marble bearing the famous inscription read by Saint Paul on an altar in Athens: "To the unknown god."

THE OECUS

Occupying the southwest corner of the house is the *oecus*, or sitting room; it can be reached from the *andron* through two doors situated at either side of the altar. The size of an *oecus*, a ceremonial room, may vary considerably, and no fixed purpose is assigned to it. Sculpture plays the primary role in this one: the soberly decorated white walls function simply as the background against which delicate compositions in stucco are set off. They are the work of Gasq, and take their inspiration from the myth of Dionysus. The piano, belonging to the master of the house, is enclosed in a beautiful chest of inlaid lemon wood; Theodore Reinach was the preeminent French expert on Greek musical notation and played the hymn to Apollo on it, a musical work discovered at Delphi in 1893.

THE BALANEION

In ancient Greece, the bath was not merely an act of hygiene but incorporated the notion of pleasure. A place for relaxation after work, the bath ended with the body being rubbed with oil. In the *Odyssey*, Homer preserves this Oriental quality of Greek baths: "A nymph led me to the baths. When the bath and perfumed oils had revived me, she presented me with an extremely handsome tunic and a splendid coat; then, leading me back into the room, she placed me on a shining seat. Another nymph came forward, carrying a golden ewer and a silver bowl, and poured a draft of cool spring water onto my hands."

Before he died in 1928, Theodore Reinach left his property to the Institut de France, to which the credit must go for the perfect preservation of this masterpiece.

In the library, books are enclosed in oak cabinets.

Opposite: The balaneion. The bath is made of veined Carrara marble.

Preceding page: The Sophocles entrance, or thyrorion,
features a cast of a statue in the Lateran Museum.

The andron, *or drawing room.*

An oil lamp and the polychrome marble in the andron.

The beams and rafters of the library ceiling
are painted with geometric interlace.

The three glassed bays between the peristyle and the andron.

Opposite: The Bird Room.

VILLA KARMA

MONTREUX

A visitor arriving for the first time on the Michaelerplatz in Vienna is likely to be struck by a corner building directly across from the entrance to the main courtyard of the Imperial Palace. This commercial building is surprising for its purity of line and graceful proportions, as well as for the beauty of the green marble used on its base and sumptuous columns.

The structure created a scandal in Vienna in 1910, and its opponents were able for a time to have construction halted. Adolf Loos (1870–1933) used classical elements, such as the marble base, a corniced roof defining the main body of the building, and columns and pilasters. In spite of these classical allusions, the building was provocative and unsettling because of the great metal lintels crowning the English-style bow windows that are built into alcoves and accentuate the building's massiveness. Windows, traditionally heavily framed, are completely naked here, except for the small window boxes Loos was obliged to add by way of compromise. This deliberate nakedness, in spite of the use of luxurious materials, marks the personal style of Adolf Loos.

It was Loos who, along with another great Viennese architect, Otto Wagner (1841–1908), introduced the modern aesthetic to Vienna, at a time when the city was still under the dazzling influence of the Secession, whose exhibition hall was then being built by Joseph Maria Olbrich. Adolf Loos defended his position in 1897 through a series of articles: "The greatness of our time lies precisely in the fact that it is incapable of inventing a new system of ornament. We have triumphed over ornament: we have learned to do without it. A new century is upon us that will see the realization of the most beautiful of promises. Soon the streets of cities will shine like large white walls; the city of the twentieth century will be dazzling and naked, like the holy city of Zion, the capital of Heaven." From the 1920s on, the modern movement would apply to the letter his precepts for the total nudity of architectural volumes.

JOURNEY TO AMERICA

When Adolf Loos finished his studies at the Technische Hochschule in Dresden, he left for England, where the Arts and Crafts movement was in full swing. But it was during his stay in America from 1893 to 1896 that he received the greatest shock—the discovery of the extraordinary Chicago School, which had been erecting metal-framed commercial buildings since 1875, their sober architectural form clearly expressing their functional purpose. Building with metal entailed such technological innovation that Adolf Loos felt justified in defining architecture first and foremost as a matter for the builder, not for the

Architect
A D O L F   L O O S

Opposite: Corner round tower, facing the lake.

designer obsessed with inventing new ornaments to replace the old.

TROUBLED RETURN TO VIENNA

As soon as he returned to Europe in 1897, Adolf Loos published a series of articles in which he proclaimed loudly and clearly the ideas he had recently had revealed to him. So began his struggle against the Vienna Secession. The Wiener Werkstätte, which had just been formed by Austrian artists to promote the rebirth of craftsmanship, seemed to him based on old-fashioned concepts and imitative of the Arts and Crafts movement. It was the Emperor Francis Joseph himself who, by sponsoring the Wiener Werkstätte, was giving new impetus to the production of ornamental and decorative craftwork. To Loos, this "art of the State" was objectionable: "And the State, whose task it is to retard the development of the people, came to the defense of ornament when it was threatened. That is in the nature of things: it is not the State's duty to encourage its functionaries to make revolutions. Thus, at the Museum of Decorative Arts in Vienna, a sideboard was exhibited bearing the title 'The Miraculous Draught of Fishes.' . . . The State may after all have been right, given that a backward people is the most easily governed. One therefore must expect the State to foster ornament, although it is a sickness. The State believes in the progress of ornament and prides itself on having provided a new source of joy by paving the way for a resurgence of 'the ornamental style'" ("Ornament and Crime," 1908). Adolf Loos was the true conscience of art at the beginning of the century, and the first to make architects the world over reflect on their position and on the true nature of their artistic and moral responsibility.

THE VILLA KARMA, 1903-4

The Villa Karma in Montreux is Adolf Loos's first building. Until then he had only renovated the interiors of apartments and stores. The architect was thirty-three years old and in full possession of his powers when his client, Dr. Beer, commissioned him to transform an old structure into a modern country house. The humor and obstinacy Loos brought to the task would help circumvent the obstacles usually raised by the establishment to any work that is original or strays from the beaten path. In its single conception for the volumes and spaces of the entire plan, the work already has all the characteristics of Loos's future projects. Loos applied a second skin to the old Vaudois farm and punctuated it with four corner towers. The original roof was removed and replaced by a roof terrace. Loos chose to plaster the exterior masonry entirely in white; for the entrance he designed a grand doorway with four fluted Doric columns supporting a straight lintel and a balcony.

From the outside, the villa has every appearance of a fortress with its corner towers and the pergola crowning the roof. The last floor, added by Loos, affords a circular walk and an exceptional view of the lake. The plans for transforming the house were made by a local firm on the basis of Loos's instructions. They were drawn up from simple sketches, and Loos had little time to correct the final plans before construction began. Loos spent a week each month for a year in nearby Clarens to oversee construction of the house. However, it was only three weeks into the project, on March 3, 1904, that a complaint was lodged against Dr. Beer, a professor of comparative philosophy at the University of Vienna, for breach of moral conduct. Beer was forced to leave Switzerland for England, then the United States, bringing construction to a halt. On October 25, 1905, Dr. Beer was sentenced to three months in jail and stripped of his title and position. Thanks to his financial circumstances, he was able to post bail and resume work on his house. Loos returned to Clarens again in January 1906. He traveled to Lyons, Geneva, Carrara, and Florence to visit marble quarries: "I am happy to be in Carrara, under masses of Carrara marble. Everything is of Carrara. Even the stakes to which the grape vines are tied are Carrara marble," he wrote on a postcard dated January 17, 1906.

In mid-March of that year Laura Beer fell gravely ill and, in profound shock at her husband's conviction, committed suicide on March 23. Relations between Loos and Beer did not start to deteriorate until the end of 1906. In early 1907 the two were ready to part ways, and Loos recommended Max Fabiani to complete the work on the Villa Karma. In the end it was the architect Hugo Ehrlich who oversaw the final stages of construction—without, it appears, betraying the spirit of the work.

THE INTERIOR DESIGN

Once past the majestic colonnade, one enters the elliptical entrance hall, its floor handsomely laid with a concentric pattern of black and white marble. Encircling the space is a high gallery, faced with sumptuous gilded mosaics. Red marble brackets support this light gallery. Incorporated into the massive front doors are the symbols for yin and yang, representing the border between two worlds, interior and exterior. As soon as one crosses this symbolic threshold, the austerity of the white plastered exterior façades is replaced by the warm luxuriance of the marble and woodwork of the interior. The gilt mosaics, the red and black marble, the amber tones of the mahogany, and the white of the Carrara marble all express Loos's love of handsome natural materials, which need only be placed and used simply.

The entrance hall and its adjoining passages form the central axis around which Loos organizes the various spaces. The dining room and smoking room both receive indirect light through the glassed-in veranda that overlooks the lake. The interior of the house is thus bathed in soft light and derives added warmth from the dark wood ceiling beams. All of Loos's talent is evident in the sequence of rooms he has created to bring in through the veranda and the library a strained and softly filtered light.

The dining room is clad in white marble, which Loos himself selected from the quarries of Carrara. The floor is covered in a checkerboard of white and black marble, a pattern picked up in the patinated metal plaques of the ceiling. All the angles of the masonry are rounded, and the architect even managed to curve the marble. Stained-glass windows filter the light, while mirrors reflect the vicissitudes of sky and water. The sumptuous doors, made of polished brass with beveled glass panes, lead out onto the gallery. The smoking room, symmetrical to the dining room, provides a restful ambience with its fireplace surrounded by majolica and its pale blue walls bathed in soft light, filtered through tinted glass.

The library is the main room on this floor. A long space, it leads to an office at one end and a pretty circular sitting room at the other. Set in the round tower, the sitting room overlooks the lake through its three large horizontal windows. The regular rhythm of the books and the black marble pilasters marks one's passage through the library. The ceiling is patterned with mahogany coffers, and Loos concealed electric lighting in the cornice. On the second floor one finds the music room, the bedroom, a lovely glassed-in gallery, and a magnificent bathroom clad in black marble. The bedroom, in the center of the house, is indirectly lit by a narrow curtained opening. Symmetrical to the bedroom is an exercise and massage room—the organization of the rooms on this floor thus follows the same pattern as on the ground floor, with private spaces in the center and more public ones on the periphery.

Dr. Beer did not live in the house for long; he chose to take his own life in 1919, in a hotel in Lucerne.

Loos's first country house defined the broad principles he would remain faithful to from then on and demonstrated his attachment to classicism: "Our culture rests entirely on Classical Antiquity and our architecture on Roman architecture—there is no helping it. Our way of thinking and feeling comes down to us from the Romans. . . . And each time small architects try to extricate themselves from the tradition, each time ornament again begins to pullulate, a master appears to remind us of the Roman origins of our architecture and to pick up the thread again" ("Architecture," 1910). The paradoxical aspect of Loos's work is that while he passes for the first modernist because of his rejection of ornament, his method of construction is deeply rooted in classical culture. Far from having any pretensions of being the first to invent a new style, Adolf Loos preferred to use classical tools; by putting them into play in a subtle and refined manner, he gave the rules a new meaning, a new spin, that is truly modern.

*The garden at
Villa Karma.*

The landing leading to the second floor.

The sitting room in one of the round towers.

The dining room of Carrara marble.

The gallery above the entrance hall.

*Opposite: The luxuriant marble and gilt mosaics of the entrance hall
are in striking contrast to the austere exterior of the house.*

The circular staircase leading to the second floor.

The black marble bathroom.

VILLA MALAPARTE

CAPRI

The home of writer Curzio Malaparte (1898–1957) is an enigmatic and fascinating work. The villa sits atop a rocky spur that rises precipitously out of the clear waters of the island of Capri, not far from Naples and Pompeii. With its red color, basic shape, and grand theatrical staircase resembling one of those Greek theaters that face the sea, the villa seems to engage in a dialogue with the gods of Olympus. The filmmaker Jean-Luc Godard made a knowing choice in using it as the set for *Le Mépris (Contempt)*, based on the novel by Alberto Moravia. "Rome is the modern world, the West. Capri represents the world of antiquity, of nature before the advent of civilization and its neuroses. In short, the title of *Le Mépris* could have been *Remembrance of Homer.*"

This work is like no other and has no identifiable style. It underwent a strange metamorphosis when the writer changed the architect's initial plan, and the result has echoes of the strange creations of the painter Giorgio de Chirico, with their metaphysical settings.

CURZIO MALAPARTE

THE FASCIST CONTEXT

"Architecture has not existed in Italy since the eighteenth century." So begins the Futurist manifesto published in 1914 by the young architect Antonio Sant'Elia, which marked the birth of the modern movement in Italy. It was not until the creation of the Gruppo 7 in 1926 that a "European" trend arose among young Italian architects turning to the works of Le Corbusier, Walter Gropius, and Ludwig Mies van der Rohe. This group was in favor of functional architecture within a regional setting, and aimed thereby at creating a national tradition in modern construction. Far from making a clean sweep of the past, as innovative German or Dutch architects were doing, the Italian rationalist school simply reformed neoclassical principles. This aesthetic avant-garde became swept up in the rise of the Fascist movement, and could not, or would not, escape its weighty influence.

Adalberto Libera (1903–1963) belonged to the generation of architects who tried, in Mussolini's Italy, to reconcile the aspirations of modern architecture with those of Fascist ideology. Libera thus participated in the Exhibition of Rational Architecture in Rome in 1928, for which he constructed several pavilions. In 1932 he designed the façade and sanctuary of the Mostra della Revoluzione Fascista in Rome.

A few major works somehow survived that confusing era, such as the famous Fiat complex in Turin (1927), designed by the architect Matte Trucco. In Como, Giuseppe Terragni built two of the most beautiful architectural works of the era: the housing complex of Novo-

comum (1927–28), and his masterpiece, the Casa do Fascio (1932–36).

LIBERA'S INITIAL PROJECT

In January 1938 Malaparte bought an enormous tract of land that included a rocky spit advancing into the sea. On the advice of Orfeo Tamburi, who was then artistic director of Malaparte's magazine *Prospettive*, he contacted the young Roman architect Adalberto Libera and sent him a few photographs. Sight unseen, and without benefit of a topographical map, Libera drew the plans for a modern villa in the style of others he had built in Ostia. He designed a large, elongated rectangle in which he situated the bedrooms; above this rustic base he positioned the living room, crowned with a succession of vaults, and, on the same level, an open terrace.

Work had already begun when, thanks to his contacts in the diplomatic corps, Malaparte was able to get a building permit—though the land was clearly unsuited to it. Construction of the villa lasted three years, as all the materials had to be transported by sea from Naples at considerable cost to the owner.

THE PLAN OF THE HOUSE: A MANIFESTO

The house is a long rectangle 26 feet (8 meters) wide by 92 feet (28 meters) long, with a corridor running the entire length, off which are the bedrooms and two bathrooms. The plan of this house was to be used again by Libera in 1940 for a housing exhibit in which the main theme was "the one-person home and studio." Thus, from an exceptional private commission, Libera created a model for an economical house, much as Le Corbusier had done with his first artists' villas. Libera avoided the traditional typology of Capri houses, which borrows from Moorish, Roman, and Gothic architectural styles, and, far from embracing eclecticism, he created a new typology, a house in the modern style that would become a virtual manifesto.

Malaparte was clearly in favor of modern architecture: as he wrote in the first volume of *Prospettive* (1937): "To express the revolutionary and imperial character of Fascist Italy, it would be absurd and ridiculous to resort to archeological reconstruction and give columns, capitals, and pompous marble catafalques the predominant role. Railway stations, markets, schools, hospitals, airports, and power stations are completely different from Greek or Roman monuments, temples, mausoleums, arches of triumph, or amphitheaters." Therefore, Malaparte's villa should not be considered a mere exercise in style but an affirmation of a controversial stance in opposition to the Italian architects

Opposite: On a rocky spur facing the Mediterranean.

who continued to turn out archaic structures in the midst of the modern Fascist revolution.

THE METAMORPHOSES OF THE PROJECT

The changes that the writer made to the architect's initial plan are quite apparent. He switched the location of the terrace from the second floor to the top of the house, keeping the base, with its bedrooms and service areas, intact. In Malaparte's plan, the large living room was placed under the monumental staircase, leaving only the writer's office in the "prow" of the rectangle. The vaults proposed by Libera disappeared, replaced by a totally flat ceiling. The addition of the monumental exterior staircase was certainly Malaparte's idea, as the innovation appears nowhere in any of Libera's drawings. This metaphysical collage immediately transformed the plan of a modern villa into a strange and unique creation. It could only have been the encounter of the house and the rock that slowly led the builder and his client to invent so theatrical an access to the large sun roof.

To reach the villa, one takes a narrow path through a pine forest, a silent, twenty-minute walk punctuated by splendid views of the sea below. The villa appears suddenly around a bend and offers one of the most arresting meetings of architecture and the sea imaginable. The visitor now follows the little path built specifically for this sad, harsh, severe villa, as Malaparte himself described it. The path leads to the foot of the monumental staircase, whose widening shape draws the visitor on, still in shock, toward the ancient panorama of the sea, bringing all of Greek mythology to mind.

By its very siting on the rock the house becomes Greek, facing the sea like those theaters of antiquity or those Roman villas fronting the shore. The initial design was purely modern and rational, but Malaparte progressively oriented his composition toward the purest classicism: a base (the rock), a shaft (the rooms) and a capital (the terrace), with the monumental staircase linking these three elements in a majestic vertical procession, a setting very much in fashion during the Fascist era. The ground floor is taken up by four bedrooms, the kitchen, and a small rustic dining room whose only furnishings are a prominent wood stove, a massive wood table, and a wood bench. An interior staircase leads to the living room, which is very large in accordance with Malaparte's wishes, 49 feet (15 meters) long by 26 feet (8 meters) wide. The floor is paved with irregular slabs of limestone, a technique the ancients knew as *opus incertum*, recalling the Roman roads that led the legions throughout the Empire. The most remarkable aspect of this room are the four enormous windows framed in red wood and reaching almost to the floor. The decoration of this room, where horizontal lines predominate, is achieved by the mere presence of a massive fireplace, whose hearth opens onto the sea. Heavy slabs of solid wood rest on fluted column sections. Off the living room are two symmetrically placed, identical bedrooms, one for the writer and the other for his "favorite." In the prow of the rectangle is the writer's study, a large room ringed with low bookcases, above which three windows open onto the horizon. There is no excess of decoration. Malaparte opted for harsh simplicity in his choice of heavy door frames and rectilinear furniture.

What makes this house one of the most emblematic works of the twentieth century? Why was there a gradual slide from modernity to antiquity? Why was the gleaming white extolled by so many modern architects rejected in favor of the red that speaks of the ancient cities buried nearby under a layer of ash? The visual strength of this work lies in the total starkness of its architecture, the choice of minimal shapes, and the absence of any anecdotal detail or explicit reference to history.

This house is the perfect example of a metaphysical architecture with ties to the atemporal landscapes of de Chirico paintings, where the characters exist enigmatically in a pure and ideal space. Here there are no references to traditional Mediterranean architecture: no vaults, arches, openwork balconies, pergolas overlooking the sea, porticoes, or verandas. There is nothing but a volume stripped of ornament, making the statement that silence is more beautiful than a swarm of useless architectural details. It took a certain courage to build a totally isolated villa on an arid rock bare of all vegetation; it was the expression of a striving for luxurious solitude.

CURZIO MALAPARTE; OR, THE ART OF FICTION

Malaparte's life in itself sums up the progress of Italy, which from the 1920s to the 1950s followed such an extreme path. In 1921 Malaparte became a member of the Italian Fascist party, along with so many of the young men demobilized right after the war. As cultural attaché in Warsaw, he embraced Fascism and participated in the march on Rome. In 1924 he founded the weekly *La Conquista dello Stato*, then became editor-in-chief of *Il Mattino*. In 1937 he created the magazine *Prospettive*, which published the major writers of the era and championed the Surrealist movement.

In 1946 Malaparte resumed his regular activities as a journalist and settled in Paris. It was only after the resounding success of his novel *The Skin* that Malaparte returned to Italy. He developed close ties to the Italian Communist party and was sent as a special envoy to the U.S.S.R. and China. In 1957 he became gravely ill. He obtained his membership card in the Italian Communist party on April 12 of that year, but died on July 19, in Rome.

A picture window.

The bedroom of the "favorite."

Opposite: A staircase resembling a Greek theater.

The floor of the living room is paved
with irregular slabs of limestone
set in mortar.

The sea is visible beyond the hearth of the fireplace.

Opposite: Antique and modern furnishings.

CONCLUSION

Modernist ideology, . . . with its Manicheism, its utopian vision of a radically new art, seems to me obsolete. . . . The idea persists that to arrive at the new, the never-before-expressed, one must rush toward the future. But is this true? Is the never-before-expressed always ahead of us? Or is it not behind us in what has been overlooked?

Milan Kundera, *Le Fait culturel*, 1980

After having made a study of artists' houses in Paris and of modernist buildings from the 1920s, I felt it was necessary to look beyond the modernist movement and try to figure out why our century has had such trouble building houses.

Le Corbusier sang the glories of his "machines for living," those units of collective habitation, and the response has been the residential housing movement that has ravaged the French countryside. The art of living, the art of dreaming one's house, is a right that has still to be fought for. As an architect, I believe it is necessary to visit the houses in this volume, which still carry a relevant message today. To build one's house is to build a dream, an environment made to one's measure, and to express one's deep personality, a part of us that is normally invisible. There are analogies between building one's own house and writing a novel, the art of which consists in telling a story.

I deplore the fact that architecture no longer tells us stories and even bases its claim to modernity on its avoidance of narrative. The houses in this volume provide evidence that dreams are fundamental to realizing the ideal House.

They tell us that the art of living is synonymous with the art of dreaming. Architects must be taught this in the schools again and learn that to construct a space is to construct a fiction, scenery for living. To the rationalists who have framed, standardized, codified, planned, industrialized, and modeled the house, I advise taking a walk through one of the exceptional houses in this volume to relearn the art of living.

Some might claim that these houses are luxury houses. I would answer that luxury is not necessarily what is inordinately expensive but what might at times be useless: the beautiful, the irrational, the mythic, the rare, the unique—everything that is opposed to the standardization of our way of life. The creators of these exceptional houses chose to make beauty their prime consideration; they were daring enough to devote their lives to creating a harmonious and emotionally stirring setting. To create beauty of this kind or a setting of this quality, one must first possess it within oneself before attempting to reconstruct it in space. The unfortunate fact about our century is that our system of building collective spaces is sealed away from the fragile and irrational process of dreaming.

The challenge of the twenty-first century will be to create harmony between our powerful capacities for production and our dreams. Then living will become an art.

INDEX

PHOTOGRAPHY CREDITS

All color photographs in this book
are by Thibaut Cuisset/Métis.

The black-and-white portraits
are from the following sources
(numbers refer to pages): Archeve
Mas, Barcelona: 59; D. R., 27, 39,
97; Fondation Théodore-Reinach:
85; Sir Thomas Lawrence/Sir John
Soane's Museum/Jeremy Butler
Photography: 7; Musée d'Art et
d'Histoire de Rochefort: 71; Musée
Horta, Brussels: 47; Roger Viollet:
17, 109